A Bypass in the Road

DEBI MORZARK HUTCHENS

BYPASS IN
THE ROAD

JOURNEY OF THE HEART

TATE PUBLISHING
AND ENTERPRISES, LLC

Published by Tate Publishing & Enterprises, LLC
127 E. Trade Center Terrace | Mustang, Oklahoma 73064 USA
1.888.361.9473 | www.tatepublishing.com

Tate Publishing is committed to excellence in the publishing industry. The company reflects the philosophy established by the founders, based on Psalm 68:11,
"The Lord gave the word and great was the company of those who published it."

Book design copyright © 2013 by Tate Publishing, LLC. All rights reserved.
Cover & Interior design by Isaiah R. McKee

Published in the United States of America

ISBN: 978-1-62902-468-4
1. Christian Living:Practical Life:Health   2. Inspiration: Motivational

13.10.22

DEDICATION

Larry, you still always know the right time to hold my hand. I love you with all my heart.

To my precious family: Mandi, Matt, John, T.J., Jason, Candice, Lauren, Marla, Faith, Griffin, Isaac, Luke, John Michael, and Christian. Thank you for going on this journey with me. You are my smile. I love you all very much.

I have been blessed to have the guidance and support of two strong women during my lifetime: my mama and my mother-in-love, two examples of unconditional love. Even when the odds were definitely not in their favor, they showed me how not to give up and stand firm in what I believed.

Sadly, when I first published this book, I could not imagine that my precious mama would not be here for the second edition. After all, she was my biggest cheerleader. Somehow, in the distance, I can still hear her rooting me on.

Patti, Steve, Vic, and Lisa, thanks for being my first friends, your unconditional love, and helping me become the best "me" I could be. This is another story in itself!

For my other family in Virginia and elsewhere, thank you for reminding me that there is no problem too big for GOD, and for teaching me to laugh, even in hard times! Distance can never keep our love apart!

To all my doctors, especially Dr. Zoe Jones, who perseveres with zeal to carry the biggest brunt of my heart journey, Dr. Greg Harold for having the discernment to know "something" was going on, and the nurses at the Perry Hospital, the Medical Center of Central Georgia, and Health Connections, thank you for always going the extra mile. How do you do it?

I would also like to thank my friends and First Baptist Church family who stood in the gap for me, held my arms up when I had no strength, and for continuing to be such prayer warriors. You truly are a hug from HIM!

And most especially, to my LORD and SAVIOR JESUS CHRIST, thank YOU for YOUR amazing grace!

₁jour·ney
ˈjər-nē (noun)
₁: an act or instance of traveling from
one place to another: An extended trip¹

For the past several-plus years, I have been on a journey of the heart, trying to find my way back to the person I was prior to my heart bypass surgery. To be honest, I do not totally want to be that person again. I pray that I have become seasoned into someone more CHRIST-like through this adventure and that others will see HIS hope in my life, even during the uncertainty. I want to touch them with HIS heart as HE has touched me.

This road definitely has not been easy, but through HIM, it has not been unbearable. There have been unexpected whips and turns that I didn't think I could endure. It has been necessary for me to grasp onto my FATHER's hand tighter than ever—each and every moment. Some people may consider this a weakness, but it is the best decision I have ever made. HE alone has become my PROVISION, my HEALER, my EXPECTATION, and my REDEEMER. HE wants to be yours, too! There is no situation impossible to HIM! So, no matter what, don't give up on your journey of the heart.

TABLE OF CONTENTS

The worst storms make the best rainbows...

"That I may publish with the voice of thanks-giving, and tell of THY wondrous works."

Psalm 26:7, KJV

A BYPASS IN THE ROAD: JOURNEY OF THE HEART

We are all on a heart journey. Paths that can tug on our very existence. Unexpected doors that open without warning, requiring us to step out of our comfort zone into uncharted waters. A job loss. Financial strain. A traffic jam when we are in a hurry. An unkind word. Sudden illness or even death. Do we allow GOD to walk with us?

FOREWORD

The past thirty-five years I have been privileged to know thousands of people who called me their pastor. Quite frankly, many of these I do not remember. But a few continue to stand out in my mind. None more so than my friend Debi Hutchens. She was and is one of the most unique people of faith I have ever known. In this book you will see what others have seen many times over the years. A woman of deep spiritual resolve, whose relationship with the Lord is both intimate and intense. At the same time you will see a woman struggling honestly with the fear and anxiety that anyone would have when facing life and death realities.

A Bypass in the Road is a powerful testimony to the sustaining presence of Christ in times of incredible trial. In this account you will find humor in the midst of heartache, peace in the face of panic, and grace sufficient for the moment of testing. This is the account of a friendship between a simple believer and the Savior who kept His word to "never leave nor forsake her."

Every life has a bypass. Not all people have faith for their bypass moments. Without faith these become times of self-destructive introspection, leading more often than not to deep and ever deepening depression. With faith however there is more than hope, there is victory that overcomes the world. Where do we turn when we face life's uncertainties? We turn to a God who loves us and has a plan for our lives. The scripture declares, "All things work together for the good to those who love God and are called according to his purpose." This book may well be the good that God has worked together from an incredible time testing. Debi Hutchens is my friend. What strikes me as more significant is that she knows my friend Jesus. Read and enjoy and let *A Bypass in the Road* be an encouragement to your heart.

Dr. Allan Lockerman
First Baptist Church, Cleveland, Tennessee
August 2007

IT'S ALL ABOUT US!

On my mother's seventieth birthday, she received an "It's All about Me!" doll. Years before, after my dad's unexpected death, she had the task of raising five children by herself. Sacrifices were made, and the road was not always easy for her. Just before this birthday, she had finished an extensive regime of chemo and radiation for lung cancer. This doll was to be a memento to Mama that finally she could concentrate on herself and what she wanted. It was all about her!

At times I ponder about our society today and me in general. We have fallen into the trap of thinking it is all about us. As we struggle, trying to climb the ladder of success, sometimes clawing our way to the top, or just keeping up with the Joneses, we have lost our ability to positively touch those we come in contact with for Him.

We are always in a hurry. Tired but restless. Forever on call. Never still. Stubborn. We've taken for granted the blessings of life and each other and do not savor precious moments we are given. We have it all, yet possess nothing when we allow ourselves to be robbed of the fragrance of relationship with Him and others because we have become so busy trying to survive the rat race.

Time is a gift, but we don't always take advantage of sweet moments that can never be retrieved again. We put off until tomorrow, but are not guaranteed it will dawn. We allow ourselves to live with regrets and miss the rejoicing. We permit life to become mundane, task-oriented, and routine, and we fail to see the preciousness of it all.

"Whereas ye know not what shall be on the morrow. For what is your life? It is even a vapour, that appeareth for a little time, and then vanisheth away" (James 4:14, KJV).

"Teach us to number our days, that we may apply our hearts unto wisdom" (Psalm 90:12, KJV).

Our quiet times with God are cluttered with many sounds and not at all quiet. God speaks in a still, small voice, but the world's volume is blaring so loudly in our ears that we can't hear Him.

We are in a pattern of the survival of the fittest and often carry the burden alone when we have an amazing Father who wants to bear the load. Somehow we have left God out of the equation all together on our journey. That is, usually until crisis comes.

Several things stand in the way today of His will for our lives: we've become creatures of comfort and habit, we seek instant gratification, and we lack genuine availability to others.

More often than not, we are creatures of comfort and habit. If we have control of our day and those around us, then we feel successful. It's a good day! However, when the road becomes unfamiliar, we struggle as we try to manipulate the situation to suit our need to be in charge. We attempt to keep plodding along at our pace to the finish line with as little discomfort or interruption as possible, becoming irritated when others or the unexpected invade "our space." Our stress levels have climbed off the chart as we clamor to achieve or be recognized.

Essentially, we thrive on instant gratification and immediate answers. We've turned into a microwave-results society, and get easily annoyed if we are delayed, even a little. Crock-pots and snail mail have become almost obsolete. Instead, we continually search for the latest "trends" we are confident will make our lives easier: instant messaging, tweets, fast foods, express lanes, cell phones, voice mail, credit and debit cards, PayPal, Blackberries, Droids, iPods, Smartboards, computers, and pagers. We eagerly pay our bills and shop on-line from the solitude of our homes. The list goes on and on.

It even seems our children are mimicking our example and have traded their childlike toys, jump ropes, crayons and coloring books for Wii's, Kindle

Fires, Xboxes, iPads, Apps, Twitter, and Facebook at younger and younger ages. You don't believe me? Just ask them.

Sadly, we are globally accessible to everyone and mentally available to no one. We've acquired so many "helpful gadgets" yet plummet further behind. We have exhausted ourselves as we try so hard to stay afloat. Our hearts have become hard-edged as we avoid opportunities for real relationships with others or our Father. It takes too much time.

Believing we are self-sufficient, we attempt to handle life on our own, again with little or no interference. We've rapidly lost our accountability to each other and our Lord, as we easily rid ourselves of unproductive associations we think will cramp our style.

Unfortunately, we've also become so focused on what we don't have that we miss the blessing of what we already hold. We carelessly toss away relationships, including those we are supposed to embrace, as we seek the "next best thing," forgetting things are supposed to be used and relationships cherished, not the other way around. Also forgetting the grass is not eternally greener on the other side.

"If you'd like to speak to someone who cares, press '1' now." Click!

In many ways, we've placed so much self-assur ance in our abilities, our titles, and the token possessions we've attained that we don't recognize God as our true provider. And, we have forgotten that He wants to go with us on this journey.

We serve an eternal, ever-present, unshakeable, loving Father who is right here with us. How it must hurt Him when we are too busy to seek His face. When we tell Him, "It's okay, I have control of this situation." Or, "I am so swamped today, Lord. I will talk with you later when it is not so crazy." Feeble excuses to the King of kings.

Like a parent walking his child to school on the very first day, God wants to take care of the hidden obstacles that pop up in our lives. He wants to clear the broken pieces from our path. He desires to hold the flashlight in the darkness. He wants us to climb on His lap during the storm. Yet, we've become so absorbed with maneuvering the outcome ourselves, we forget that we have access to His help all along as we struggle with our frustrations. It is usually not until we are knocked on our back by the unexpected that we realize He has always been watching ready to lift us up.

God also wants us to take our focus off the world and the momentary pleasures it offers and look to Him. When we won't obey, because of the false security we've place in ourselves or how much "stuff" we've obtained, sometimes He must allow the uncertainty of the storm to draw us back closer to Him. You know, when the rug is abruptly pulled out from under us and there's nowhere else to look but *Up*. Or the circumstance plummets so quickly out of our control, we finally realize that true lasting hope comes only from Him and not ourselves.

Sometimes, it is only necessary for our Father to simply nudge us with a mere "rain shower" to get us to turn our eyes back to Him. Other times, because of our stubbornness, prideful hearts, sin, or disobedience, it takes a "tsunami of atomic bomb proportions" to get our full attention. Regardless of the size or the lesson in the storm, He is there with arms outstretched towards us!

One thing for sure, storms will continue to occur throughout life, but our God is faithful through each one. He does not waiver!

He is the God of the tempest. The Alpha and Omega. The Beginning and the End. Our Shepherd. And although we time and again walk through shadowy dangers in the valley, *He is always with us*. We are not alone!

I have found, it is the darkest valley experiences that strengthen our relationship with our Father and pull us closer to Him like a magnet to a piece of metal.

So, will we be spiritually-minded or self-absorbed? Seek or shrug off His plan for us? Receive or rebel at the direction He is taking our lives? Garner or grit our teeth at the lessons He tries to teach us? Become better or bitter during the storm?

The choice is ours! The God of the mountaintop is also the God of the valley. His love never changes!

"Take heed, and beware of covetousness: for a man's life consisteth not in the abundance of the things which he possesseth...For where your treasure is, there will your heart be also" (Luke 12:15, 34, KJV).

"For what shall it profit a man, if he shall gain the whole world, and lose his own soul" (Mark 8:36, KJV).

"But know this, that in the last days perilous times will come: For men will be lovers of themselves, lovers of money, boasters, proud, blasphemers, disobedient to parents, unthankful, unholy, unloving, unforgiving, slanderers, without self-control, brutal, despisers of good, traitors, headstrong, haughty, lovers of pleasure rather than lovers of God, having a form of godliness but denying its power...always learning and never able to come to the knowledge of the truth" (2 Timothy 3:1-7, NKJV).

MY HEART JOURNEY OR BEING KNOCKED ON MY BACK BY THE UNEXPECTED

In the past, I have let my life become cluttered with the world's expectations for me. At times, I have pushed myself into the unrealistic trying to please everyone I come in contact with. My church. My job. My family. My friends. I have allowed the waters to overflow me. I have given in to discouragement, although I mask it well with a smile. I have often stretched myself so far to succeed that I have frequently sacrificed myself. I have given place to pride, the fear of failure, and what others think with no regard to my Father and what He wants for my life. And I have wasted valuable time.

I have tried to live up to the image others have of me and have forgotten how I am created in His image. But God always has a way of reminding us that we are His.

Does this sound like your journey?

"I cried unto the Lord with my voice; with my voice unto the Lord did I make my supplication. I poured out my complaint before Him; I shewed before Him my trouble. When my spirit was overwhelmed within me, then Thou knewest my path" (Psalm 142:1–3, KJV).

"As a father has compassion on his children, so the Lord has compassion on those who fear him" (Psalm 103:13, NIV).

I was in Debi's pre-Christmas rush mode at work, finishing tasks I felt were urgent to complete before Christmas break, and became a little irritated when Dr. Harold's office insisted I come in for blood work before refilling my prescription for cholesterol medication. Going to the doctor for silly blood work was the last thing on my list. Praise God that he had strict rules for reissuing medications, and his "insistence" probably saved my life.

During this visit, while making small talk, I casually inserted how walking from one end of my building to the other resulted in my arms and sometimes chest tightening up. I was also a little more tired than usual. "Boy, I am really aging," I rationalized without taking a breath. "I have four grown kids and expecting my fourth grandbaby in the summer. It has been a hard year with my mom's lung cancer battle. I also need to drop a few pounds. Can I have a B-12 shot?"

I am not sure what the "light bulb" moment was for him, but my doctor ordered an EKG just to be on the safe side. Not thinking anything was unusual,

I had my EKG and was surprised when he said he was setting-up an appointment immediately with the heart specialist. *But it is almost Christmas and my kids are coming home.*

A few days later, early morning on December 14, I checked into the Georgia Heart Center at the Medical Center of Central Georgia for a recommended heart catheterization, accompanied by my husband, Larry. As one of the nurses escorted me to the prep area, I happened to notice that she was wearing a W.W.J.D.: *What Would Jesus Do?* bracelet. When I asked her about it, she eagerly told me she was a Christian. Her bubbly personality was a comfort to me, and it seemed as though we had been connected for a lifetime, and through Him, I knew we were joined for an eternity.

Before she left my room, she also shared two other meanings of W.W.J.D.: *Why Would Jesus Die?* Then backwards, *Devil Just Won't Win!* I needed to be reminded that I already had the victory through what Christ had done for me. I had no doubt God had placed this particular nurse in my life at that moment, and through her words, a prayer, and a hug, any apprehension I was having about being at the hospital quickly faded.

"Preserve me O God: for in Thee do I put my trust" (Psalm 16:1, KJV).

Two techs finished my prep process and reassured me this was a common procedure. I felt silly in my open-back hospital gown and IV. No, this was not my plan for the day, and I was anxious to get everything over and find the nearest Christmas sale.

Once prepped, Larry was allowed to stay with me in my "holding cell," and I shared the events up to that point. Our former youth pastor from church arrived just before I was wheeled into the catheterization lab. As he prayed, I was reminded again God was in control. I hoped that Larry was as reassured as I was and would not worry. I knew that he was not accustomed to seeing me in such a vulnerable position. I was relieved that God sent someone to pray with us. You can never have too much prayer!

When I arrived in the cath lab, much welcomed Christmas music sounded from the speakers. Still I recounted in my mind how many more presents were not purchased. Although we would be getting off work after the 20th, I would have a few days until my daughter and her family flew in from California, and my boys came home. *There is still time,* I thought. *I just have to get through this catheterization.*

The lab staff was dynamic and instantly put me at ease as they described the procedure while meticulously placing electrodes on my arms, legs and body. The catheter, a long thin tube, would be inserted in a blood vessel in my groin area above my right leg through a small incision. The tube would be guided into my heart and a contrast medium dye would be injected through the catheter while pictures of my heart and arteries were taken. With the dye procedure, the extent of blockages or narrowing would be seen. I could even watch the screen if I wanted. *Hum, imagine that!*

I was given a dose of a relaxant and told by the anesthesiologist some people actually fell asleep during the procedure. We laughed after several doses of relaxant were administered in my IV, and I was still perky and fa-la-la-ing. With a smile, he stated that I was not a cheap date.

The heart cath adventure seemed harmless enough. Not expecting anything but maybe a stent or two at the worst, my attitude was, *The sooner I get this catheterization done the sooner I can return to normal and focus on Christmas. Where's the nearest mall?*

However, the mood of the room quickly changed to somber. I was surprised to hear that I would need four heart bypasses as soon as possible for some serious blockages. In spite of everything, my first thoughts were consumed with the upcoming holiday and the un-purchased, perfectly wrapped presents that were not under my tree. I have a June Clever reputation to live up to and even wear the pearls. *Who's going to get the house ready? There are goodies to be baked and a turkey to be stuffed. I still haven't killed the fatted calf yet!*

And what about my office? My bosses and others depend on me. I thought of the strategic stacks of purchase orders and unfinished reports waiting for my return. *Who would finish them?*

"Definitely not a good time for heart surgery. Can't this be postponed?"

How absurd I must have sounded as I pondered if surgery was really needed so quickly.

Surrender for me is a hard concept, but adjectives like "a ticking time bomb" and "massive heart attack" made me realize that there was an urgency to my surgery. Thus, with a fearless face and smile, I accepted the inevitable and gave in to the diagnosis. I would be a good soldier. Well, maybe.

Now it was time to let Larry and the kids know. *Where is my brave face so they won't know how scared I really am?*

Larry and I have been married for over thirty years. Throughout the years, we have faced many trials and victories together. We have truly become one flesh and balance each other well. I am a talker; he is quiet. He is musically talented and plays several instruments. I have trouble playing the radio and can't hit a correct note when I sing. I make "joyful noises," but not to anyone around me. When I am at my weakest, he is strong. When he is down, I am full of joy. In fact, he sometimes accuses me of thinking everything is a joke. My joy can occasionally be aggravating. Just ask him!

It seemed surreal to hear my heart doctor explain to him that I was destined immediately for bypass surgery. My heart broke as I watched his demeanor change to sadness, but I tried to keep smiling. As required after catheterization, I was laying very still flat on my back, a big challenge for me, but necessary to avoid any bleeding. I couldn't wait until we could hold each other. Only a few more hours to go.

During the silence, I remembered the two extremely naïve, scrawny sixteen-year-olds in early love. Larry routinely came by Kenny Burgers, the fast-food restaurant where I worked on the weekends and walked me home each evening. Clothed in my uniform, minus the hairnet, wearing the perfume of splattered grease from the burgers and fries, hand-in-hand we would leisurely walk down the long road to my house with no cares in the world. Just wanting to be together. Nothing spectacular according to the world's standard, but everything to us. And we dreamed big about our future together.

Marrying young at twenty, we ate our fill of deer-meat soup, peanut butter, and broccoli to get by. We were content in spite of our lean days during college, although pressures pushed us hard at times. Still, God always provided. He was our foundation and carried us through many storms.

After Larry's graduation from Virginia Tech, we began our family and moved away from the comfort zone of our home and family in Virginia. Together, while discovering uncharted territories, we grew more as one in Him as we carefully navigated the many bumpy roads that lay ahead of us.

Back in the quietness of my hospital room, I thought about a poem my younger sister, Patti, had written and presented to us during a surprise party in honor of our thirtieth wedding anniversary a few years earlier titled "Holding Hands and Walking."

Surrounded by our whole family, we relived the triumphs and hardships of our story:

> *This journey that we're on began when we were very young.*
> *Our days were full of youthful stuff like flirting glances and laughter.*
> *But our friendship developed into a special bond...*
> *As we began holding hands and walking.*
> *We longed to spend every moment together,*
> *And soon we became one.*
> *A promise made, a promise kept...*
> *To continue holding hands and walking.*
> *We struggled through the college years And dreamed about our future.*
> *Wondering if our dreams would come true...*
> *Still holding hands and walking*
> *Before we could blink our eyes we welcomed our first baby.*

*The changes continued as we packed up and
moved far away…*
Always holding hands and walking.
We adjusted to our new life quickly,
*Although we were homesick for
our family and friends,*
*We soon realized that good things would
come about*
*By living on our own…our grip got a little
tighter…*
While holding hands and walking.
*There were transfers and promotions, and
three more babies came.*
*It was during this time away that our life
was truly changed,*
As we found our blessed Savior—who said,
"Come follow Me…
Keep holding hands and walking."
Even when we're apart,
*There is no distance so great that we will
not be connected.*
*As my hand is forever imprinted
with yours,*
And your hand with mine…
*As if we were holding hands
and walking.*
*Our journey as husband and wife has lasted
thirty years.*
*We've experienced great joys together, as
well as times of sadness.*

Sometimes it's hard to look back
at where we've been,
But we know that's what prepares us for
our tomorrows...
Forever holding hands and walking!

At this moment, while dreading the looming dark cloud hanging over us and anticipating the impending storm, we were still holding hands like the two inexperienced kids we once were. Even now wanting to be together and scared by how quickly our lives could change, both of us clung to the Lord and tried hard to blink back any tears that threatened to fall.

I was relieved when my daughter-in-love, Candice, called and said she would contact our son, Matt, at work, and our daughter, Mandi, in California. Because our two youngest sons, John and T.J., were finishing the semester at the University of Georgia, we opted to wait until after they were done to share this news with them.

Larry needed to make some other phone calls, and I was finally alone to face my demons of fear. I sought God as never before. I pleaded with my Father to somehow strengthen us and intervene during this time of uncertainty.

Mandi soon phoned and said her husband, Jason, had managed to change her plane reservations. She and our grandbabies would be leaving within the hour to fly home to Georgia. How I praised God for helping them come so quickly. *What a comfort our family will be for Larry and me,* I thought. *Things don't seem as bad when we are with one another. Like hot coals, we all burn brighter together.*

> For I am poor and needy, and my heart is wounded within me. Help me, O Lord, my God: O save me according to Thy mercy. That they may know that this is Thy Hand; that Thou, Lord hast done it...I will greatly praise the Lord with my mouth; yea, I will praise Him among the multitude. (Psalm 109:22, 26–27, 30, KJV)

INCLUDING GOD IN THE EQUATION: FINDING HIS PURPOSE IN PAINFUL TIMES

I allowed my mind to wander to another hospital stay quite a few years earlier after we were all involved in a serious car accident. Our children were rather young then, and, praise God, no one but myself sustained an injury requiring hospitalization. I was driving our car and received a large head wound and bad concussion from the full impact. After Larry left to tend to the children, for several hours it was necessary for a nurse to stay with me at all times.

With my head stitched and packed in ice, even with a concussion, talking came easily for me. Actually, talking always comes easy to me. I told the nurse that I did not experience any pain when the two other cars involved in the accident crashed into the driver's side of the door where I was sitting. I was knocked out immediately upon impact and could have easily woken up in Glory.

At first I became concerned when I saw the tears begin to fall from her eyes. But the blessing of our accident became very apparent as she slowly began to share how she had been diligently praying that God would somehow show her if her son had any pain before dying in a car accident a year before mine. The police had tried to reassure her that her son died instantly, but she found no comfort with their empty words.

Through my sharing I experienced no pain during our car accident, she finally found the peace and comfort for her son's death that she desperately sought. God used our car accident to relay hope to someone else hurting. What if I had not shared my mishap with her?

There are so many people looking for the hope we profess in our lives, and many times we do not share it with them. We are so busy concentrating on our own "woe-is-me" moment that we ignore others around us and don't take advantage of opportunities He places in front of us.

"But sanctify the Lord God in your hearts: and be ready always to give an answer to every man that asketh you a reason of the hope that is in you with meekness and fear" (1 Peter 3:15, KJV).

I began to compare my upcoming bypass surgery with this past hospitalization experience. *Okay, Lord, what do You want me to do? Where is the good You promised? In Romans 8:28 it says, "All things work together for good to them that are called by God." This*

*does fall in the 'all things' category, right, Lord? While I
am here, who do You want me to touch for You?*

I did not realize what a miracle this supposed
inconvenience would turn out to be, or how many
special people God would place in my path. What
could have been meant for my harm would be a
blessing beyond measure. For the first time in a
long time, I slowed down and let my Father take my
hand, and I was not afraid!

> Fear thou not; for I am with thee: be
> not dismayed; for I am thy God: I will
> strengthen thee; yea, I will help thee; yea,
> I will uphold thee with the right hand of
> my righteousness…That they may see,
> and know, and consider; and understand
> together, that the hand of the Lord hath
> done this." (Isaiah 41:10, 20, KJV)

HEART DISEASE: THE NUMBER ONE KILLER OF WOMEN

According to the American Heart Association[2], heart disease is the number one killer of American women. One in three women will develop heart disease. We enter a higher risk if there is anyone in our immediate family with early coronary heart disease: a blood-related parent, sister, brother, or child.

My family history of heart disease does not only include my maternal and paternal grandparents and siblings diagnosed with mild to moderate coronary disease, high cholesterol, or high blood pressure, but my dad, my brother, and my mom—all whom suffered heart attacks.

My dad passed away at thirty-six and my brother followed at thirty-eight, both from their first massive heart attacks. Ironically, my dad died while on an "important" out-of-town business trip after stating he had too much work to finish before returning to the doctor for some necessary tests. His busy-ness cost him his life, and sadly, he never made it back home.

Fortunately, my mom survived her first two mild heart attacks in her early sixties after seeking medical attention immediately as her initial symptoms appeared. The odds appeared against me, but my Lord was not.

In addition, researching these numbers could help save your life:

- Normal blood pressure[3] should be equal to or less than 120/80;
- Total cholesterol[4] less than 200 mg/dl;
- LDL cholesterol (lousy cholesterol—clogs the arteries) less than 100 mg/dl;
- HDL cholesterol (heavenly cholesterol—clears bad cholesterol from the arteries) for women greater than 60 mg/dl;
- Triglycerides less than 150 mg/dl;
- Your ideal body weight; and
- Exercising[5] 30 minutes per day/5 days per week = stronger heart muscle.

I felt okay most of the time, so I disregarded the symptoms of tightness in my arms and chest and excessive fatigue, justifying why it was okay to ignore these warning signals. Again, I blamed them on stressful circumstances at work or home and promised myself I would get off the couch and exercise in the evening to get back in shape.

Even though five years earlier I had been diagnosed with a mild mini-stroke (TIA) from a blood pressure surge and was prescribed a blood thinner, blood pressure medication, and cholesterol medication, I failed to make any dietary and life changes that possibly could have helped me avoid bypass surgery. Like my dad, I was always hard at it!

According to my doctor, the Plavix (blood thinner) was probably a big factor in what had saved me from experiencing a heart attack. There is no doubt it was only by God's grace that I did not become a statistic, and I am thankful that He opened the doors to the help I needed.

"'For I know the plans I have for you,' declares the Lord, 'plans to prosper you and not to harm you, plans to give you hope and a future'" (Jeremiah 29:11, NIV).

"Behold, I am the Lord, the God of all flesh: is there any thing too hard for me?" (Jeremiah 32:27, KJV).

"My times are in Thy Hand…" (Psalm 31:15, KJV).

WILL YOU MAKE ME A BIG GLASS OF LEMONADE FROM THIS LEMON?

The fear of facing the unknown when told you need a heart bypass is somewhat overwhelming, and I was also slightly discouraged when I was told the surgery would not be performed for three days due to the blood thinner I had been taking. It would be discontinued and would be replaced with a Heprin drip through my IV until my surgical procedure.

Imagine previously moving at speeds that exceeded the Road Runner cartoon and then being informed it is too dangerous to leave the hospital prior to surgery because you need to be monitored. This was a before-surgery quandary, and visions of sugarplum fairies danced wildly in my head as I pondered all the things that remained undone for the upcoming holiday.

Words like *unfair* and *bad timing* occasionally reared their ugly heads, but God sent unexpected angels to lift me during my wait, and to my amazement they were not always those who I anticipated to come to my rescue.

We all have expectations and mine were that the people closest to me would rally around Larry and I, particularly because of the uncertainty of this serious surgery. Surprisingly, some of my closet friends stayed away during this time partly out of disbelief that I was a candidate for bypass surgery. After all, just a few days before I had been prancing up and down the hallways at work and the aisles of Wal-Mart fa-la-la-ing the rapidly approaching Christmas break, attempting to spread some Christmas cheer to my co-workers and others I came in contact with.

I was so hungry for prayer but soon discovered those I thought would spend time praying with me found it somewhat uncomfortable to do so. To them I was the least likely to be stuck in the hospital awaiting heart bypass surgery.

> Is any among you afflicted? Let him pray. Is any merry? Let him sing psalms. Is any sick among you? Let him call for the elders of the church; and let them pray over him, anointing him with oil in the name of the Lord: and the prayer of faith shall save the sick, and the Lord shall raise him up; and if he have committed sins, they shall be forgiven him. Confess your faults one to another, and pray for one another, that ye may be healed." (James 5:13–16, KJV)

On the outside I appeared to be in good health. On the inside, a battle was raging in my heart. However, God was totally aware of what was going on! This was not a surprise to Him.

We tend to look on the outside appearance, but God looks at the heart. Had He not opened the door for intervention from my doctor, the outcome could have been very different for me and my family.

"Man looks at the outward appearance, but the Lord looks at the heart" (1 Samuel 16:7, kjv).

For a brief moment, I allowed the enemy to plant seeds of discouragement and guilt. I worried I wouldn't be able to make this Christmas special for my family, and that I also would be leaving my office in a lurch. Although I acted perky while others were around me, there were times inside I pleaded with the Lord that my diagnosis would be a mistake and I would receive a reprieve from the doctor or the governor for this "sentence."

Friends and family questioned their own health and quizzed me about my symptoms as if they could be the next victims. I found myself reassuring others and challenging them to go to their doctors for a check-up. After all, heart disease is a silent killer and I wanted them all to be checked.

God understood my heart and fears. He sent just the right people at His perfect time to deliver His message of hope and encouragement. An unexpected army of prayer warriors came at various intervals to stand in the gap for me, willing to walk with me in this battle! Through His Word and their prayers, I began to find the victory I desperately sought.

Somehow, we needed to make lemonade out of this lemon. More than anything, I wanted God to be glorified in my life through this unplanned heart adventure, and I was reminded that I needed to surrender and lay my surgery at His feet.

"Carry me, Father," I begged.

"Two are better than one…if one falls down, his friend can help him up" (Ecclesiastes 4:8–10, NIV).

"Bear ye one another's burdens, and so fulfill the law of Christ" (Galatians 6:2, KJV).

"And I will bring the blind by a way that they know not; I will lead them in paths that they have not known: I will make darkness light before them, and crooked things straight. These things will I do unto them, and not forsake them" (Isaiah 42:16, KJV).

WHERE WILL I WAKE UP?
HERE OR GLORY?

The evening before my bypass, my family packed my hospital room like an overstuffed Volkswagen. Our grandbabies climbed on my bed for a makeshift picnic with Nana. I worried that my unplanned surgery might have a negative impact on their lives, and wanted to make sure that my hospital experience would not be alarming for them.

The room was filled with lots of laughter and hope as each small child interrogated me with lots of "What's that?" and "Why?" questions, which I tried to answer as optimistically and simply as possible.

Would they remember me if I did not survive the surgery? What legacy would I leave? Did they know how much I cherished the Lord and them?

Goodbyes are difficult, and finally everyone, including Larry, had gone home to get some much-needed rest before my "bypass adventure" the next morning. Alone, I began creating a book for them to share with one another while in the waiting room. In my small, hand-sized composition book, I began writing Bible verses that pertained to the heart.

There are many! Following quite a few pages of verses, I felt led to write a note to each child and my husband. I just wanted them to know how special they were to me. I also wanted to remind them that regardless of where I would wake up after surgery, I would be okay. In my heart, I pleaded with God to give my family strength no matter what and use the small book I had made them.

"For to me to live is Christ, and to die is gain" (Philippians 1:21, KJV).

Only imagining how difficult the waiting room duration would be, I decided to close my book with games including twenty-nine questions of "Who did/said this in the Hutchens family?" which I knew would make them laugh and hopefully would take some of the sting from their wait. I challenged them to share memories and look forward to making new ones together. I also reminded them how God had always carried us in the past and of all the blessings He would continue to pour on our family in the days to come.

> "Hear my cry, O God, attend unto my prayer. From the end of the earth will I cry unto Thee, when my heart is overwhelmed; lead me to the Rock that is higher than I. For Thou hast been a shelter for me, and a strong tower from

the enemy. I will abide in Thy tabernacle for ever: I will trust in the cover of Thy wings. Selah" (Psalm 61:1-4, KJV).

God provided very sensitive and caring nurses at the hospital. Before my midnight food deadline, I was surprised with Hershey kisses and a cup of fresh coffee. It was like receiving a chocolate kiss from Him. Several nurses came in my room during the night to give me words of encouragement and to answer any questions I had.

The night quickly turned into early morning, and I was prepped for my extreme makeover. My son, John, arrived as they were getting ready to wheel me to the surgical floor. It was particularly cold in the hallway, so the orderly sent him back to my room to grab a blanket for me.

While John was absent, an unknown man came up to my gurney and clinched both my hands. He began praying with incredible Pentecostal power one of the strongest prayers that I had ever heard, asking God to place me in His protection in the bosom of Abraham. After his prayer was complete, he drew so close to my face that I could feel his warm breath on my cheeks. He informed me I did not need to be afraid. I would survive my bypass. Then, as quickly as he came, he was gone.

I still do not know who this man was, whether a hospital clergy or an angel. I only know that my Father sent him to me as a personal reminder of His hope. God was in control and His presence was so real to me. Most importantly, I was not afraid! Had I just "entertained an angel unaware" (Hebrews 13:2, KJV)?

My relaxants really began taking affect as I was wheeled to my family apprehensively waiting in the surgical area. We laughed as my mouth dried out and my lips rolled up over my top, protruding front teeth. I imagined I looked like the talking horse, Mr. Ed. *"Oh Wilbur!"* I was so glad that my last minutes prior to surgery with my family were full of laughter. And I was not afraid. Well, maybe just a little…

> "O Lord God, I cried unto Thee, and Thou hast healed me. O Lord, Thou hast brought my soul from the grave; Thou hast kept me alive. Weeping may endure for a night, but joy comes in the morning. Lord, by Thy favor Thou hast made my mountain to stand strong… For Thou hast turned for me my mourning into dancing: Thou hast put off my sackcloth, and girded me with gladness. To the end that my glory may sing praise to Thee, and not be silent. O Lord my God, I will give thanks unto Thee for ever" (Psalm 30:2–3, 5, 7, 11–12, KJV).

BEING INDUCTED INTO THE ZIPPER CLUB!

A couple of surgical nurses in a brightly lit, rather chilly room greeted me. When I first caught a glimpse of the narrow table where my operation would be performed I laughed. "You think my body is going to fit on that skinny table?" Fortunately for the staff, the anesthetic quickly took affect and I finally was silent and still.

It was time for my CABG, pronounced "cabbage," coronary artery bypass graft surgery. According to my surgeon, an approximate eight-inch incision would be made down the center of my breastbone. Once the bone was separated, the doctor would be able to reach my heart. I would be placed on a heart-lung bypass machine, which would assume the duties of my heart and lungs by permitting the circulation of my blood/oxygen throughout my body. My heart would be lifeless and nonfunctioning, minus any blood activity.

While on the heart-lung machine, for the first time, I would be unable to speak at all. The surgery would take about four to six hours. A world's record of quietness for me!

One of the nurses had explained the night before that my brain functions would also be turned off during surgery. I asked that she make sure they turned everything back on once I was in recovery. I need all the help I can get, especially with my brain! Ask anyone!

My blood would be re-routed through four vein grafts detouring by my blocked arteries. After surgery, I would sport three stitched incisions on both numb legs where unusable veins had attempted to be harvested. Other sources of grafts would be taken from my chest and stomach to allow the much-needed blood to flow completely through my heart without being blocked. When the bypass surgery was completed, my chest opening was wired, stitched, and even super-glued to close the incision.

Lucky for me, my day-job did not depend on an unblemished chest or flawless legs. What a scar souvenir I would now proudly wear as a memento of my heart adventure and how Christ had carried me during this trial. Daily reminders of the scars He bore for me at Calvary.

"My heart is fixed, O God, my heart is fixed. I will sing and give praise" (Psalm 57:7, KJV).

My body became the domicile for many wires, tubes, and monitors: a ventilator through my mouth, oxygen tube in my nose, bladder catheter, chest tube to drain blood and fluid from around the heart, an IV to route fluids back in my body, a pacing wire in case of an emergency and my heart needed to be restarted, and monitoring devices for heart rate and blood pressure. A port had also been inserted in the carotid artery in my neck so that blood samples could easily be taken or injections of medicine given.

I had more devices growing out of me than Bayer had aspirins. Frankenstein had nothing on me!

LAUGHTER FROM THE CVICU

Together, Larry and the children were escorted to the CVICU, Cardiovascular Intensive Care Unit, once I had been stabilized. It was hard for my family to see me so sedate with equipment protruding from every nook and cranny of my unresponsive body. The ventilator was making my chest rise and fall in steady rhythm, and I was very puffy from all the fluids and extremely pale. Most alarming to them, however, was seeing me extremely quiet as they listened to the subtle sound of the machine breathing for me. This was not the picture of the mom who normally was in control and making a silly response or jingle to an adverse situation.

Prior to surgery, I had made a pact with my kids and several of the nurses to first, make sure my right foot was out from underneath the covers (don't ask); and second, once I started coming to and becoming aware of my surroundings, removing me from the ventilator as soon as possible.

Years ago, I had watched my grandmother panic and distraughtly fight being on a ventilator while coming out of a coma. I did not want to put my family through that awful experience. Revisiting memories of her suffering tormented me each time I thought of her last days.

Coming to, I vaguely remember taking my right hand and pointing to my mouth in anticipation of having this apparatus removed. I eagerly obliged as the command was given to relax and blowout, as I finally felt the invasive tube slide from the depths of my throat. What a liberating feeling to be able to breathe on my own again. I praised Him for not allowing me to panic while on the ventilator; now it was out, and I was breathing freely! I never appreciated breathing this much before.

Due to the anesthetic, for quite a while, I was in and out of consciousness, attempting to talk, and entertaining my family with insights both real and stranger than fiction. He does call us to be a "peculiar" people, doesn't He?

I experienced such awe that my mighty Father had pulled me from the depths of despair that I could not help but praise Him to everyone. I was so thankful. For my family. My life. His love. You name it, I was thankful. Isn't this how we should be all the time? Why do we forget this?

When the nurse told me I was doing a good job, I told her it was because of what God had done and asked her if she knew Jesus as her Lord and Savior. Although still under the effects of the anesthetic, I was on His mission. My kids saw that even in hardship, I wanted to know if she knew my Lord.

Disclosing His hope was an important part of my life, and I regretted many opportunities I had let slide by in the past because I thought I was too busy to take time to stop and share.

If we are the salt of the world, during times of crisis, shouldn't our lives taste even saltier? How else are those around us going to become thirstier for Him?

My family was ushered out of the room so I could rest. When Mandi returned, she noticed that I was staring intently at a blank screen on the wall. Asking what I was "watching," I told her Paula Deen was frying chicken and it tasted so good. We still laugh about my fried chicken non-episode. There would be no more fried chicken in my lifetime.

After a few days, once I was stable and completely aware of my surroundings, I was allowed to return to the regular cardiac nursing floor.

"A merry heart doeth good like a medicine: but a broken spirit drieth the bones" (Proverbs 17:22, KJV).

"Then was our mouth filled with laughter and our tongue with singing…the Lord hath done great things for us; whereof we are glad" (Psalm 126:2–3, KJV).

"Let the saints be joyful in glory; let them sing aloud upon their beds" (Psalm 149:5, KJV).

LIONS, TIGERS, AND BEARS...COUGH, COUGH!

Being returned to a room on the normal cardiac floor was a small victory for me. Although I experienced some discomfort similar to being hit hard by a semi-truck or an overeager linebacker, it was encouraging to have visitor restrictions lifted and be allowed to move from the confines of my bed to a chair.

The nurses made sure I was quickly on my feet and taking several small excursions down the hall each day. They explained that walking was an important part of my healing, and I was in a hurry to get back some semblance of normal.

I can always find something to laugh about. During one of my earliest treks around the nurse's station, two male nurses supported my IV station as they guided my clumsy, wounded body down the seemingly long hallway. What a sight! We were walking at a pace that would give any snail confidence of winning the race. I laughingly chanted, "Lions, tigers, and bears, oh my," while slowly parading past the doors of several patients and their families, holding my hand high imparting the pageant wave. I could hear the laughter coming from each room as I passed by.

Arm in arm, our entourage finally conquered the long corridor and returned to the safety of my room. I was worn out, as probably the nurses were too! An accomplishment to be repeated over and over again!

Coughing was another essential task towards recovery. My surgeon presented me with a bear-shaped pillow to cushion my chest while coughing. This was probably one of the most expensive stuffed animals I have ever received. Neiman Marcus would be proud! The nurses explained to me that coughing and breathing deeply would help prevent fluid from building in my lungs.

My appetite was nil-to-none, and family and friends tempted me with delicacies like ice cream, milk shakes, and slushies. You name it, we tried it. My taste buds, however, would not cooperate with these once treasured delights, and everything tasted like the top of a styrofoam minnow bucket. I ate only because I had to. What a change! Finally a diet that works!

Not wanting to be incarcerated any longer than necessary, I coughed! I walked! And, I ate!

THERE'S NO PLACE LIKE HOME!

The Saturday evening before Christmas, I was finally going to be released from the hospital. I had been clad in a hospital gown and tubes for ten days, and now, tubeless, sporting a new pair of pajamas and a *big* smile, T.J. and our four-year-old grandson, Griffin, wheeled me from the confines of my room as Larry left to get our escape vehicle. Griffin held tightly to my hand in innocent excitement. Nana was actually going to come home. He waved and shouted, "Merry Christmas!" to the nurses and pranced like one of Santa's elves as we made our way to the elevator. What a time of celebration!

A rush of emotion overtook me as I was buckled in the backseat of the car. At last, I was going home. I liked the sound of that.

The twenty-some mile ride back to Perry seemed like an eternity. "Are we there yet?"

I praised God for getting me this far and vowed to never take anything for granted again. I had been given a second chance. What a blessing to be alive! When did the sky get so blue?

Like the ending from *It's a Wonderful Life*, upon entering my front door and being greeted by my precious family, I knew that whether or not I had finished my Christmas shopping this year would not deter the holiday from being exceptional. There's no place like home!

"A new heart will I give you, and a new spirit will I put within you: and I will take away the stony heart out of your flesh, and I will give you a heart of flesh. And I will put my spirit within you, and cause you to walk in my statutes, and ye shall keep my judgments and do them..." (Ezekiel 37:26–27, KJV).

"As for me and my house, we will serve the Lord" (Joshua 24:15, KJV).

"Now be pleased to bless the house of your servant, that it may continue forever in your sight; for you, O Sovereign Lord, have spoken, and with your blessing the house of your servant will be blessed forever" (2 Samuel 7:29, NIV).

A CHRISTMAS TO REMEMBER

In Christmases past, I have been the one responsible for each intricate detail. The presents. The meals. The decorations. The ambiance. You name it, I did it. In fact, I usually did it so well with a flair that sometimes I was worn out before I could appreciate the real meaning of the holiday. Many times, much to my regret, Christmas and survival became synonymous as I scrambled to make the holiday "special" for friends and those in my family.

Much to my amazement, Christmas was going to happen, and this year, others jumped at the chance to share in organizing the festivities without my help. It's true. We are replaceable!

Larry finished the shopping. Candice completed the task of wrapping. Matt and Mandi, along with their Grandma Betty and Aunt Karen visiting from Virginia, cooked up a passel of delectables for breakfast and a Christmas dinner that would make Martha Stewart smile. Much to the delight of Isaac, Griffin, and Faith, John even donned a Santa suit and passed out the presents.

John and his new wife, Lauren, presented me with an ornamental replica of the Operation Game.

They had replaced the patient's face with a picture of mine. The room was filled with laughter as the tongs were pressed and "my nose" lit up. Laughter is the best medicine…for all of us.

The message of Christmas took on a new meaning this year as we all celebrated what Christ's birthday meant to each of us. Although the hours leading up to the merriment were not perfect, this Christmas would be the best and not forgotten!

We were together. Whole. A family. Our happiness did not rest on the perfectly wrapped packages under the tree, but the blessing of the babe born in the manger. Come, let us adore Him!

> "And lo, the angel of the Lord came upon them, and the glory of the Lord shone round about them: and they were sore afraid. And the angel said unto them, Fear not: for, behold, I bring you good tidings of great joy, which shall be to all people. For unto you is born this day in the city of David a Saviour, which is Christ the Lord…Ye shall find the babe wrapped in swaddling clothes, lying in a manger. And suddenly there was with the angel a multitude of the heavenly host praising God, and saying, Glory to God in the highest, and on earth peace, good will toward men" (Luke 2:9–12, 13–14, KJV).

IF YOU CAN'T SAY ANYTHING NICE, DON'T SAY ANYTHING AT ALL!

Several days after my arrival home, a home health-care nurse called and asked if I had experienced any depression since my bypass. She told me depression was a common occurrence following heart surgery and insisted that I jot down the phone number of a behavioral specialist that worked with the insurance company. I eagerly replied back to her that so far I had not faced the demon of depression and was finally on the road to recovery.

I was taken back when she adamantly stated it appeared to her that I was not dealing with my condition because I was too happy. I responded that I was a happy person. Ask anyone who knows me! Call me crazy, but this was usually how I handled adversity. I proceeded to ask for her home phone number and laughingly stated that I would give her a call at home if I became depressed. That abruptly ended our conversation.

But the enemy jumped on this seed of doubt unknowingly planted by this healthcare representative. What if I wasn't dealing with my surgery? What if I never fully recovered? What if I was separated from my family? Who would take care of them? On and on my mind played ping-pong with itself as question upon question reared its ugly head.

There is so much power in our words. I thought about other people, who by the sway of suggestion might actually be prone to depression if this negative seed was planted in their minds. Could it cause them to descend on a downward spiral? Would they have support at home? Would they know to seek His help?

God reminded me how important what we say to others is, and I prayed that my careless words had not torn someone else down in the past.

I was thankful I had a positive support base from my family and my friends. I was also grateful that I had a Father who loved me so much to lift me out of the miry clay of despair.

"Even in this struggle—use me, Lord, to touch someone for you," was my humble plea. "And please, let me get back to normal."

"I waited patiently for the Lord; And He inclined to me, And heard my cry. He also brought me up out of a horrible pit, Out of the miry clay, And set my feet upon a rock, *And* established my steps. He has put a new song in my mouth— Praise to our God; Many will see *it* and fear, And will trust in the Lord" (Psalm 40:1-3, nkjv).

A VIEW OF LIFE FROM THE BACK OF AN AMBULANCE

One afternoon, eight weeks and several doctor visits following my bypass surgery and after almost two weeks of cardiac rehabilitation, I began to experience discomfort in my chest radiating down my arm and up my neck. Praise God, T.J. had come home from college because he did not have a class on this particular day. I believe he did not come home by chance and God used him to save my life.

Not learning my lesson the first time as well as I thought, I began justifying the pain as probably from my incision. After all, it was cold outside and my chest was reacting to the chill. When will I get it?

I took a pain reliever hoping the sensation would go away, but T.J. was not convinced and, with strength I did not realize he possessed, encouraged me to call my cardiologist, *now.* I was surprised when she told me to get to the local emergency room immediately, and we decided it probably was also a good idea to let my local family physician know what was going on.

My mind flipped back to a chapter in my life where I was the one sitting by the bedside of one of my sick children praying for their quick recovery. Now the tables were turned as T.J. and one of his friends took on the role as caregivers and drove me quickly to the ER. "You don't look very good, Mom."

Like a bad classic TV repeat from *Sanford and Son,* I was ushered into a holding area where many questions were asked and my blood pressure was taken. "Elizabeth, this is the big one. I'm coming to join you, honey."

Finally, I was admitted into the ER and given an EKG, blood work, chest X-ray, and an IV of nitro and blood thinner. My blood work would be done every few hours to check my enzymes. More poking and prodding. I had become a human pincushion. How I hated this setback, not just for me, but also for my family.

Once my doctor arrived, Larry and I were in disbelief to hear that I was actually experiencing a heart attack. An enzyme level in my blood work showed an elevated count. It would be necessary for me to spend the night, and yes, once again be monitored. Can I sing my rendition of Patsy Cline's "Crazy"?

The next morning, I was placed with all my paraphernalia in the back of an ambulance once again destined for the Medical Center. While on this latest trek up I-75, the Lord began to speak to my heart through three visual lessons from the back of the ambulance.

First, you can only see where you have been out the small back windows in the ambulance. God used this as a reminder of where He has brought me from so far. It is necessary to know where you have been to know where you are going. There have been other times in my life when the journey was as unclear. He had not let me down yet, and this reaffirmed I could trust Him to get me through this trip of uncertainty.

Secondly, you can't see who's in the driver's seat, so you have to trust the driver by faith to get you to the proper destination. The trip was totally out of my control. There have been other instances in my life's journey when He drove me over unknown roads. I could not see who was in charge, and by faith, had to believe that He was directing my route.

Lastly, it's up to the driver alone to maneuver through the traffic, dips, and ruts in the road, no matter how rough. I was strapped in, lying backwards on my gurney, and could not control the steering wheel or see what was ahead. This reminded me that God has been navigating just fine without my help and interference. Nothing is too hard for Him! I was totally impaired to do anything except pray and trust my Father through the bumps in the road. And I had to surrender—again—to this fact. Letting go and letting God!

"Be still, and know that I am God" (Psalm 46:10, KJV).

"A man's heart deviseth his way: but the Lord directeth his steps" (Proverbs 16:9, KJV).

GOD'S PLAN B

What a déjà vu moment as I arrived in the catheterization prep area on the seventh floor of the Medical Center. Several of the techs remembered me from my last visit eight weeks earlier. I attempted to joke with them that I thought I was going to the spa, but inside I was filled with dread and a deep fear that I was afraid to convey. Again, God knew my fears.

"This time, I want lots of drugs," I nervously chuckled when I was wheeled into the cath lab. I was apprehensive to hear the results of the cath, and I felt being on "cloud-nine" would make hearing the outcome a little easier—no matter how temporary.

My cardiologist was not available for the process, so her partner would do the procedure. I remarked how young he looked. Almost like Doogie Houser. When I think about it, actually, lots of doctors now are younger than I am.

"Please Lord," I pleaded, "only a stent or two if necessary." My mind wandered to Larry alone in the waiting room. No more bad news please. Then

I overheard the doctor say that two of my bypasses had collapsed. Yikes!

At that instant, I felt like all my well-made plans, my health, my future, everything I placed my hope in were escalating out of control. I was drowning. *What do I do now? Actually, Father, what do You do now?*

Although the enemy was saying, "You are crushed. Nothing good will come out of this," the Savior was saying, "Calm down, Debi. I am in control. Nothing will happen to you without going through Me first. Hang on to Me."

What a battle! Again, I was out of my comfort zone, alone on the cath table, separated from those I loved and cared about. Had my life really counted for the Lord? Or had I been so busy playing the game, I missed out on His perfect will for my life? What a mess this had become.

The cath team opted to repair only one of the arteries by angioplasty and inserting one medicated stent. It was determined that there was too much risk to fix the other collapsed bypass at this time. Once more, I had to lay this setback at my Father's feet. He was in charge of the outcome, and I reminded myself how much He loved this frail, broken child!

I recalled a terrible summer thunderstorm when I was a small child. My dad was sitting very attentively in his recliner listening to the storm warnings blaring across our small black and white television set. The wind was howling, the lightning was flashing, and the thunder was responding with ominous roars. The rain and hail were steadily pounding on our frame house as the storm fell upon us, but I found comfort that my dad was still up, protecting us from the thunderstorm. As long as I knew he was there, I felt very safe in my bed, covers pulled firmly over my chin, that is, until the lights went out and I could no longer see him. I immediately jumped out of my bed and ran as hard as I could into the dark room. I can still hear myself crying out, "Daddy, Daddy," in the darkness and feeling his strong arms pulling me up onto the safety of his lap and wrapping around me tightly until I felt secure again from the storm and fell asleep. In spite of what was happening outside, wrapped in the shelter of my dad's arms, I felt safe and no longer worried about the deluge, no matter how loud it was.

Now a new storm was hitting the frame of my house, and again I could hear myself calling, "Daddy, Daddy," but this time, it was my Heavenly Father I was crying out for. Once again, I jumped in my Daddy's lap like never before needing Him to hold me tight and surround me with His arms until the storm was over!

THERE IS NO TIME TO WAIT: TAKING THE SIGNS OF A HEART ATTACK SERIOUSLY

Remember, you know your own body and your family history. Women do not have to feel the same crushing symptoms as men to be diagnosed with heart disease. It is better to find medical help and be wrong about having a heart attack than to wait hoping symptoms will subside. If you are having a heart attack and do not seek medical assistance quickly, this could result in permanent heart damage or death.

A heart attack begins when the coronary arteries are blocked or narrowed by a clot or plaque and an adequate supply of blood and oxygen cannot flow through the heart muscle. As this happens, heart muscle dies and the ability of the heart to pump blood to the rest of the body is reduced. This is why rapid action is crucial to reduce the amount of damage and scar tissue to the heart. If untreated, larger areas of heart muscle die and heart failure can occur.

Get to the hospital immediately, especially if you have family history of heart disease and you experience:

- Pain in your chest, shoulder, one or both arms, tooth, back, stomach, neck or jaw;
- Shortness of breath;
- Tightness, squeezing, fullness, or heaviness in your chest;
- Sweating with chest pains; and/or
- Feeling sick, lightheaded, or nauseated.

An excellent source, the American Heart Association Web site, www.americanheart.org states, "although some heart attacks are sudden and intense, where there is no doubt of what is happening, most heart attacks start slowly with mild pain or discomfort. Often people affected aren't sure what's wrong and wait too long before getting help."[6]

Consequently, you may not know what is going on and dismiss early symptoms as I did. Don't be afraid to ask questions or get help quickly. *Your life or the life of someone else could be in jeopardy if you do not seek immediate help!*

I couldn't begin to imagine how this last point would be once again driven home so dramatically in my life until a few years ago while staying with my mother following a supposedly "simple surgery" to remove a growth between her skull and brain, and insert a titanium plate in her forehead. The removal of the growth seemed to go without a glitch. Although she experienced some confusion after the procedure, Mama stayed in the hospital only a few days and was eager to return to her home and recover.

A home healthcare nurse had come to make an initial visit the following morning to determine if she was able to maneuver the twelve steps from her living room to her bedroom and also perform simple household tasks. No problems were evident during this observation.

After lunch, we both took a much needed nap snuggled close together just like when I was a small child. The only sounds were "oldies" streaming from a radio kept near Mama's bed.

Shortly after we had awaken, my teenaged-niece Sarah, had just arrived and come upstairs to visit her Granny. Mama was lying in bed singing along with one of the melodies filling the air, even swaying her arms to the rhythm of the music with a huge grin on her face. From time to time, Sarah and I would giggle as we tried to chime in with her. Nothing seemed to be amiss. After a short visit upstairs, Mama decided she was strong enough to continue our conversation downstairs from her recliner.

When she first caught a glimpse of herself in a mirror at the top of the stairs, she laughingly commented about her disheveled "hairdo" caused by the once cockeyed bandage-wrap that slid from the top of her recently shaven head, revealing an invasive incision, staples and stitches from ear to ear. It was great to hear her laughter and ours!

I vividly remember navigating each stair carefully with my arm wrapped securely around my mother's frame, taking each step at a snail's pace, although I knew deep inside, she really wanted to do it by herself.

Half-way down, Mama suddenly stopped and said she just needed to sit and rest. There was no visible sign that anything was wrong, but by the time she came to a resting position in the middle of her stairway, she was gone. Without any struggle or indication she was in any pain, she passed into Glory cradled in my arms. That simple.

Sarah immediately dialed 911 upon hearing me urgently cry out, *"Mama, Mama!"*

Although members of the rescue squad arrived very quickly and persistently tried to resuscitate her, nothing could be done to bring her back. Ironically, the cause of death, more than likely, a massive heart attack, after we had placed so much emphasis on the growth inside her head.

For a long time afterwards, I pondered if she had experienced any distress beforehand and had possibly dismissed it, and I questioned repeatedly why she did not tell me so I could seek help.

How could we be laughing together right before this happened? Was there something I had missed? My heart panged as I tried unsuccessfully to seek answers while dealing with jabs of guilt, her loss, and my broken heart.

I cannot drive this point strongly enough: it is extremely dangerous to ignore early warning symptoms of a heart attack and not get help immediately! It is not worth the risk.

My only comfort was the assurance that Mama knew Jesus as her personal Lord and Savior. If not so, there would have been no time for her deathbed conversion. She was gone in a blink of the eye.

We didn't find out until after her death the meningioma had been a benign growth. Oddly, had Mama not had the surgical procedure, I would have not been in Virginia with her when she passed away. I was the first of her five children to meet her at birth, and I was also the one to hold her as she passed into Glory!

"Death has been swallowed up in victory. Death, where is your victory? Death, where is your sting? Now the sting of death is sin, and the power of sin is the law. But thanks be to God, who gives us the victory through our Lord Jesus Christ" (1 Corinthians 15:54:57, HCSB).

"Precious in the sight of the Lord is the death of his saints" (Psalm 116:15, NKJV).

JESUS CALMS THE STORM

Following my heart surgery and complications, ver and over, alone in the quietness of my home, I searched my Bible and urgently sought His healing in my life, at times becoming a little anxious for this part of my story to be complete. Yet He continued to remind me of other storms He had calmed in the past with just a word, both in my life and the lives of others.

"And the same day, when the even was come, He saith unto them, Let us pass over unto the other side. And when they had sent away the multitude, they took Him even as He was in the ship. And there were also with Him other little ships. And there arose a great storm of wind, and the waves beat into the ship, so that it was now full. And He was in the hinder part of the ship, asleep on a pillow: and they awake Him, and say unto him, Master, carest thou not that we perish? And He arose, and rebuked the wind, and said unto the sea, Peace, be still. And the wind ceased, and there was a great calm. And He said unto them, Why are ye so fearful? how is it that ye have no faith? And they feared exceedingly, and said one to another, What manner of man is this, that even the wind and the sea obey Him?" (Mark 4:35–41, KJV).

While Jesus and the disciples were crossing the lake to the other side, an uncontrollable squall arose. Right away, the disciples nervously panicked as the waves pounded into their vessel, tossing them to and fro. Incredibly, Jesus was in the back part of the ship sound asleep during all the havoc. Fearfully running to find Jesus and urgently waking Him up, they expressed what we all say to God when we get in trouble, "Don't You even care that we are all going to perish? There's a storm going on here."

Arising from His sleep, speaking just a few words, Jesus calmed the storm but also scolded the disciples for being so fearful and having no faith. After all, they forgot Who was in the boat with them.

How could they doubt how much He loved them? They walked with Him. Heard His words. Witnessed His miracles. Yet, while in the midst of their own storm, they became afraid, forgetting His hope in their lives.

The whole experience the past several weeks was definitely new territory for me, and I knew I could not face it on my own. No, this absolutely was not the ending I expected from this chapter of my story. As a consequence, like the disciples, I sometimes fearfully wanted to jump out of my boat as the waves of this illness lapped over its sides, forgetting He was in the boat with me. "Help me, Lord," I pleaded over and over as I held on to Him with all my strength.

I would not be returning to work as soon as I had planned. Cardiac rehab was now on hold. Plus there still was the lingering possibility that I would have to go through another cath procedure to correct the other collapsed bypass or worse.

"Mine eyes are ever before the Lord: for He shall pluck my feet out of the net. Turn Thee unto me, and have mercy upon me: for I am desolate and afflicted. The troubles of my heart are enlarged. O bring me out of my distresses. Look upon mine affliction and my pain and forgive all my sins...I put my trust in Thee...I wait on Thee" (Psalm 25:15–21 KJV).

"Be anxious for nothing: but in every thing by prayer and supplication with thanksgiving let your requests be made known unto God. And the peace of God, which passeth all understanding, shall keep your hearts and minds through Christ Jesus" (Philippians 4:6, KJV).

God had another plan! A more perfect one! Now, it was time for me to rest, heal, and trust. Not being anxious for anything. Sometimes easier said than done. Yet again, I needed to go back to the Potter's house. This raw, broken piece of clay needed to be remolded and reshaped by the Master's strong, skillful hands.

"But now, O Lord, Thou art our Father; we art the clay, and Thou our potter; and we all are the work of Thy hand" (Isaiah 64:9, KJV).

Realizing how quickly the outcome could change, I constantly bathed my healing in prayer. Not just for myself, but for my family and those around me. He is our Deliverer. Our Constant during the unknown. Our Transformer. Our Great Physician and Healer. Our Rest.

"As for me, I will call upon God; and the Lord shall save me. Evening, and morning, and at noon, will I pray, and cry aloud: and He shall hear my voice" (Psalm 35:16–17, KJV).

I desperately needed someone to bind with me in prayer, so I wrote an email to Christian Broadcasting

Network's prayer line at www.cbn.com requesting prayer for God's will for my healing. An up-lifting message of hope followed from CBN's prayer partner, Elaine:

> *We want to encourage you today concerning the burdens you shared with us. Look up with great hope to the Lord your God!*
>
> *The Bible says that God is able to do abundantly more than you can ask or imagine; all things are possible through Him! Praise the Lord, we know this is true!*
>
> *We also know the Lord has a divine purpose for each one of us, a plan for our lives that only He can foresee. As you pray in the authority of the name of Jesus Christ and call on the Spirit of God to empower you and help you to pray, boldly ask the Father for a miracle of healing.*
>
> *Keep praying and keep asking, praying always in the direction God's Spirit leads you. Stand in confidence on the promises He gives you as you read Scriptures.*
>
> *Be willing to receive and accept His answer as He reveals it to you, looking not to the circumstances for confirmation, but to the understanding the Lord Himself will bring to your heart.*
>
> *We join with you to praise the name of Jesus Christ, for the Lord your God, Who moves*

even the greatest mountains by the power of
His Spirit, will be faithful to you![7]

God was aware of my struggle. He heard my heart-cry. He knew I felt like I was alone in the wilderness. From the beginning, nothing about me has been hidden from Him. And He used His Word to remind me over and over again that He was here with me:

"Whither shall I go from Thy spirit? or whither shall I flee from Thy presence? If I ascend up into heaven, Thou art there: if I make my bed in hell, behold, Thou art there. If I take the wings of the morning, and dwell in the uttermost parts of the sea; Even there shall Thy hand lead me, and Thy right hand shall hold me. If I say, Surely the darkness shall cover me; even the night shall be light about me. Yea, the darkness hideth not from Thee; but the night shineth as the day: the darkness and the light are both alike to Thee. For Thou hast possessed my reins: Thou hast covered me in my mother's womb. I will praise Thee; for I am fearfully and wonderfully made: marvellous are Thy works; and that my soul knoweth right well. My substance was not hid from Thee, when

I was made in secret, and curiously wrought in the lowest parts of the earth. Thine eyes did see my substance, yet being unperfect; and in Thy book all my members were written, which in continuance were fashioned, when as yet there was none of them. How precious also are Thy thoughts unto me, O God! how great is the sum of them! If I should count them, they are more in number than the sand: when I awake, I am still with Thee" (Psalm 139:7–18, KJV).

God also used a special friend who came to my home unexpectedly to minister to me in a unique, humbling way. Teresa knocked on my door one morning when I had felt the rug had been pulled out from underneath me. I was in a battle with myself, very discouraged that I would never get my life back as it once had been. I had not shared this discouragement with anyone in my family or any of my friends. Yet, God was still wiping each tear I refused to cry.

Teresa was a woman with a definite mission as she toted a zebra-striped towel, foot soaker, creams, and all the extras to wash my feet. The aroma of her laughter suddenly filled my house, overtaking the stench of sadness that reigned only a few moments before. Imagine, a friend being so in-tuned to God, willing to humble herself and minister in such a special way to me.

Of course, my spirit was filled with thanksgiving for her obedience to Him. We discussed whether some of the disciples had laughed because they were ticklish when Jesus washed their feet.

How Jesus must have loved His friends, the disciples. These ordinary men had walked with Him on the dusty roads. They ate together. Prayed together. Shared together. Maybe even told fishing stories or carpentry secrets to one another. They lifted Him up, and sometimes they let Him down. How it must have grieved Him to know the road that lay ahead for each of them. And yet, He ministered to them in such a humbling way, preparing them for their journey to come. The King of kings, and Lord of lords, humbly bent down and washed their feet.

> "Ye call Me Master and Lord: and ye say well; for so I AM. If I then, your Lord and Master, have washed your feet; ye also ought to wash one another's feet. For I have given you an example, that ye should do as I have done to you. Verily, verily, I say unto you, The servant is not greater than his lord; neither He that is sent greater than He that sent Him. If ye know these things, happy are ye if ye do them" (John 13:13–17, KJV).

Through Teresa's submissive example to humbly minister to me, I was challenged to be this kind of friend to others in the future. I wanted to be known once again for my compassion and not someone who wallowed in despair. I yearned for others to see Jesus in me and not this heart problem.

"A man that hath friends must shew himself friendly: and there is a friend that sticketh closer than a brother" (Proverbs 18:24, KJV).

"Greater love hath no man than this, that a man lay down his life for his friends" (John 15:13, KJV).

"Praise be to the God and Father of our Lord Jesus Christ, the Father of compassion and the God of all comfort, who comforts us in all our troubles, so that we can comfort those in any trouble with the comfort we ourselves have received from God" (2 Corinthians 1:3–4, NIV).

How I longed to experience His complete healing. To hear His voice say it was going to be okay, and soon I would be whole again. I prayed to be free from this storm and proclaim the power of His victory. To laugh, share, and just be me without any recurrences. I hated being labeled by my infirmity when people talked or thought of me. I wanted my life to be about Him.

Again, I sought His hope through His Word. Then I met this woman, with great faith despite the odds against her...

> "Now a certain woman had a flow of blood for twelve years, and had suffered many things from many physicians. She had spent all that she had and was no better, but rather grew worse. When she heard about Jesus, she came behind Him in the crowd and touched His garment. For she said, "If only I may touch His clothes, I shall be made well."
>
> Immediately the fountain of her blood was dried up, and she felt in her body that she was healed of the affliction. And Jesus, immediately knowing in Himself that power had gone out of Him, turned around in the crowd and said, "Who touched My clothes?" But His disciples said to Him, "You see the multitude thronging You, and You say, 'Who touched Me?'"
>
> And He looked around to see her who had done this thing. But the woman, fearing and trembling, knowing what had happened to her, came and fell down before Him and told Him the whole truth. And He said to her, "Daughter, your faith has made you well. Go in

peace, and be healed of your affliction'"
(Mark 5:25–34, NKJV).

Imagine being caught in an immense crowd, looking for the One who could end your sickness. Desperate faith. Having already exhausted every other resource and treatment available. Nowhere else to turn.

She was also a woman with a definite mission. This "certain" woman toted her label of illness for twelve years. Branded unclean because of an issue of blood, others avoided her. Unable to go into the temple. Broken physically, spiritually, and monetarily, she hopelessly looked for her deliverance from this curse. And day-by-day, her condition was growing worse.

Then she got it! If only she could touch the hem of the Great Physician's garment she would be made whole again. She did not let the thick crowd stop her. She intently pushed herself through the horde to get closer to Jesus. Immediately when she touched the Hope of all hope, her issue was gone. After years of suffering, she was completely healed!

Although pressed on every side by the crowd that sought Him, Jesus felt her touch and asked the disciples, "Who touched my clothes?"

He already knew all about her. As she fell down before Him, trembling with awe, she recognized her Savior and what He had done in her life. I only imagine His compassionate eyes looking down at her and thinking, *This is my beloved daughter in whom I am well pleased.* Her faith had made her whole.

Moreover, this was my prayer—*please let my faith be strong enough to make me whole.* Oh, to see His compassionate eyes.

"Now faith is the substance of things hoped for, the evidence of things not seen...But without faith it is impossible to please Him: for he that cometh to God must believe that He is, and that He is a rewarder of them that diligently seek Him" (Hebrews 11:1, 6, KJV).

STANDING IN THE SHADOW OF THE CABG (CABBAGE) PATCH

If you had asked about my life prior to December 2006, more than likely I would have shared about my job for the Houston County Board of Education, where two of my favorite tasks were setting-up conferences and training sessions, and ordering new materials and equipment to help students become "successful lifetime learners." Afterward, if you had not yet had a chance to make your quick escape, I would have proceeded to share endless tales with excitement about my family and my relationship with the Lord.

Life was good! As the song goes, "I could bring home the bacon and fry it up in the pan....I was WO-MAN."

Not only could I multi-task at the office under two supervisors, but I was also pretty good around my house. I guess you could have called me an over-achieving-Jill-of-all-trades.

However, three months after surgery, still sporting physical trophies down my chest and on both legs, plus one collapsed bypass and a stent in the other, I eagerly returned to work, attempting to perform tasks once effortlessly carried out in the past.

In spite of being chemically drowned by my regimen of daily medications, including my nitro-patch, simple exertions such as handling boxes of professional books would consequently trigger bouts of angina pain and shortness of breath, causing an uneasy vulnerability from once routine duties. Each day, my lack of stamina and strength becoming more and more evident to others and myself as I literally would collapse into exhausted, deep sleep once returning home.

During this struggle, I daily sought Him, praying He would show me His will for my life. Regrettably, following a short "stent" of returning to my job, in my "heart" I knew He was allowing this door to be shut, and I humbly admitted defeat and surrendered to early disability retirement from what had been my comfort zone where I felt in charge and confident.

As the final souvenirs and personal effects of my professional identity for almost fourteen years were carefully placed in the last box, I tearfully said good-bye to co-workers who had become a very important part of my daily life. Coffee buddies. Sisters. Comrades. Confidants. Office family. Closing this familiar and once comfortable chapter and heading home from work for one last time. No longer one of the girls. Sadly, although not deliberate, eventually to be forgotten as each one moved on to survive their own hectic schedules without me.

Their dance cards full of handsome prospects as they effortlessly jitterbugged, while mine seemed virtually unsigned while I attempted to execute a slow waltz on a separate dance floor.

As in other times of uncertainty, in the quietness of my house, this time, I urgently sought to find God's will for this unfamiliar path. Re-examining my life to see what God would have me do with the idle time now found on my hands. After all, the last time I was June Clever, clad in pearls, anxiously anticipating Ward's arrival home, previously occurred when our four grown children were all small.

Now, alone within the walls of our empty nest, unsure what lay ahead. Larry leaving early each morning, and I, pondering my new-found role, trying not to waste any part of the day God had given me. Realizing the blessing of this precious yet fragile gift ... time! Also contemplating ways I could I touch others for Him through my uncharted journey. Trusting somehow He would provide just the right path.

In Jeremiah 29:11 (NIV) it says, "For I know the plans I have for you," declares the Lord, "plans to prosper you, and not to harm you, plans to give you hope and a future."

How I had to trust Him!

Wholeheartedly, I began to seek Him further through His Word. There had to be something else in His purpose for me. Then I discovered how God oftentimes uses our brokenness as a springboard for His utmost calling for us.

He had finally gotten my full attention. The sounds of the world were no longer blaring in my ears. It was quiet in my house and also in my heart. I had turned my eyes upon Jesus right where I needed to be!

It started subtly when someone approached me about my availability to share my "heart story" to a group of ladies by asking an uncomplicated question, "Do you ever speak?"

Laughingly I replied, "Well, I talk" (little did she know actually all the time).

And with that simple statement, God began to unlock an unexpected door for me to share my heart at a ladies conference, not for my glory, but for His!

He was slowly beginning to reveal to me His plan, for such a time as this, to step out of my comfort zone to reach unfamiliar people in unfamiliar places. He wanted to use my surrendered heart, my gift of gab, a love for others, and the sudden closing of a door to unveil a new path for my life. Not for my harm, but for His purpose and glory.

Praise God, He was going to use my disability and make it His-ability. To transform my biggest imperfection and develop it into His opportunity to touch others for Christ. And although I was humbled, I was also somewhat concerned He had chosen me.

The "enemy" oftentimes tried to remind me I was not a trained speaker. I was just a talker. What did I really have to say that could make a difference in someone's life?

I was also struggling regularly with health issues. It didn't take much to exhaust me and any exertion tended to cause shortness of breath and angina pain. Would His strength really be made perfect in my weakness? Would I commit or cringe at His new call on my life?

It was not until God reminded me how others were looking for hope in a world filled with hopelessness that I realized He had used my heart surgery and the complications which ensued as my training ground, to enable me to reach out to those who needed encouragement and comfort during their own storms. Through my own personal adversity and the comfort GOD had provided me through His Word and those HE sent to lift my arms in battle when I felt I couldn't go on, I became more aware of the conflicts of others around me and I wanted desperately to share His hope with them.

Through His Word, God confirmed He wasn't concerned about my ability, but rather my availability to His calling. I had accepted God's call on my life. I would try to no longer be distracted by my heart condition, but devoted to His will for my life, even on the bad days.

As I began to share the testimony of what God had done during my physical and spiritual heart journeys with those He placed in my path, His Spirit began to reveal to them the hope I had in Jesus Christ was real and not just empty conversation. I struggled just like they were struggling and could relate to their journey. I could sincerely share His comfort because I had also received His comfort ... actually I was still receiving it!

> "Blessed be the God and Father of our Lord Jesus Christ, the Father of mercies and God of all comfort, who comforts us in all our troubles, so that we may be able to comfort those who are in any affliction, with the comfort with which we ourselves are comforted by God. For as we share abundantly in Christ's sufferings, so through Christ we share abundantly in comfort too" (2 Corinthians 1:3-4, 6, NKJV).

Recently, God reiterated His call on my life through this verse while on a much needed sabbatical to North Georgia after receiving a new, uncertain diagnosis (but that's another book). Larry and I decided that we would visit nearby Amicalola Falls, the highest waterfall east of the Mississippi River and also labeled as one of "Georgia's seven wonders," although I am not sure what numbers one through six are.

We had never been there before and on the spur of the moment, decided to go for a leisurely walk, not knowing what to anticipate, although a web-page for the falls stated "a relaxing and rejuvenating return to nature awaits you." Exactly what we both needed: relaxation and rejuvenation!

So with tennis shoes laced, slowly we began our ascent up the trail towards the falls taking in the beauty of His creation throughout the woods. The abundant mix of rhododendron, dogwood, pines, hardwoods, wildflowers, and a flowing stream in the midst coming down the mountain were breathtaking. Definitely painted by the Master's hand.

Many others, including the elderly, small children, and dogs seemed to make their way with ease up and down the winding path. "How hard could it be?" I thought, as I observed apparently happy faces coming and going in both directions.

As we moved closer towards the falls, I was getting a little worn and slightly winded, so Larry grabbed my hand and began to pull me as he walked. We laughed as we held hands and shared memories of other climbs we had made early in our marriage almost effortlessly. My how things had changed. No longer were we the spry youngsters that could maneuver a trail effortlessly, and beads of sweat drops started streaming down my forehead saturating my bangs and face, as I pondered, "Wonder how much further the falls are?"

The paved path abruptly came to an end transforming itself into a steep "beast" of wooden and steel steps that appeared to have no end as I looked up finding no view of the falls. Doubt began to envelop me as I suddenly let go of Larry's hand and peered at the looming warning sign at the base of the steps: 175 STEPS DIFFICULTY: STRENUOUS.

"Larry," I said dreadfully, "I am sure I cannot continue. The sign says difficulty strenuous and you know the word strenuous and my health do not mix well together. Just go on without me," I coaxed.

"Can you just try?" he asked with a look of child-like disappointment.

So with a grimace on my face, try I did. I felt breathless and definitely out of shape after climbing what seemed to be a thousand-more steps, but in reality we had only gone up two more levels.

Once more, I strongly echoed, "I am really sure I cannot continue," as the sweat drops now burned my eyes while my heart raced and my mind kept revisiting the ominous sign below, causing the beauty of the setting to blur exceedingly.

And yet again, his response, "After you rest and drink some bottled water, we can continue."

Argggg! (My thought)

So I spitefully scaled another round of steep steps until I reached the next resting station. Stubbornly I plopped down on the bench and appealed, "I positively can't climb any higher. Why else would they put a warning sign up unless they expected some people to fall out? Remember my heart disability? You definitely do not understand!"

Upon those words, an older woman wearing a knee brace, who couldn't help but overhear us, stopped on her trek down the steps and said to me, "I totally understand your hesitation. I also have a disability. Look up towards the top of the steps. You can catch a glimpse of the base of the falls. You are almost there! There are only two more levels, each with a place to stop and rest. It doesn't matter how fast you reach the falls. Just take it slow like I did."

"But my husband wants to go to the top of the falls," I replied gloomily while pointing at Larry. "There is absolutely no way I can do that."

"The beauty of the waterfall is at the bottom of the cascading falls, not at the top," she encouraged. "The bottom of the falls is the prize. I promise you can do this if you take it slow like I did," she repeated.

After I thanked her, she headed back down the mountain.

She could understand my plight. She had been where I had been. This nameless encourager had doubts on her climb, too, but she had eventually made it to the falls.

After a short rest, I felt a boost of unexplained energy. I placed my focus up towards the bottom of the falls and no longer on the recollection of the sign below. Imagine my celebration when I finally made it. Arms raised in victory just like Rocky Balboa!

Although Larry loves me, he had not experienced weakness and reservation like I had climbing to the falls. He could not understand my struggle or hesitation. It took someone who had gone through a similar situation to reassure me and get me to refocus on what was important.

What a powerful visual object lesson God had shown me for the purpose of my heart journey: helping me be a better encourager to others while sharing my own similar struggles and the victory He had given me during my storm.

"I will lift up my eyes to the hills—
From whence comes my help?
My help comes from the Lord,
Who made heaven and earth. He will not allow your foot to be moved;
He who keeps you will not slumber.
Behold, He who keeps Israel
Shall neither slumber nor sleep.
The Lord is your keeper;
The Lord is your shade at your right hand.
The sun shall not strike you by day,
Nor the moon by night.
The Lord shall preserve you from all evil;
He shall preserve your soul.
The Lord shall preserve your going out and your coming in
From this time forth, and even forevermore" (Psalm 12, NKJV).

MY HIDING PLACE

Several years ago, without her knowledge, I was led to pen a poem in honor of my youngest sister, Lisa, who has Multiple Sclerosis.

One of the strongest individuals I know, she never seems to complain. She always thinks about the other guy, and never meets a stranger because of her huge compassionate heart. Like me, she is a talker!

Lisa does not like to dwell on her journey with MS, and many people do not know her daily battle as she still manages to effectively serve her family, her church, the ladies ministry, her children's school, their sports activities, and her community. She is the dynamic mother of two teenagers, Megan and Day, and a wife to Tim. Most importantly, she is sold out to Jesus!

Lisa gives herself daily injections of medicine to help control her symptoms and also for three days each month, as an outpatient, she receives an MS IV "cocktail" of steroids and other mystery meds. The hospital staff loves her and takes extra special steps to make sure she is comfortable during her IV treatment. Yet she makes you feel it is not about her!

We live several states away from each other and during a bad flair-up, she expressed how wonderful it would be if I could be in Virginia with her. I told her that I *was* there and directed her to the Poetry. com web page to the poem I had written for her sometime back and had never told her about:

MY HIDING PLACE

A storm rages on, eroding the soul of the
one in its path,
Weakening this body with
fear in its wrath.
"Help, Daddy," I cry in my fear of the
storm.
He lifts me to safety and cradles me
in his arms.
His strength gently wraps around his frail,
broken child;
As a powerful shield, but also so mild.
He speaks comfort, but makes no sound.
The perfectness of His love abounds.
At this moment, all fears depart.
His unconditional love soothes
my wounded heart.
"I am your strength, your peace in this
hour.
Your hiding place, healing
fear with My power."

God planned just the right time for me to share this poem with Lisa. A time when it would mean the most in her life. Why are we amazed that He cares about even the smallest details in our lives and is constantly preparing a way for us? His timing is always perfect.

Incredibly, He reminded me how He was still cradling me in His arms during this season of storm in my life as I reread this poem.

Storms in life are to be expected! They usually arrive unanticipated at inopportune times, like when you are exhausted and that dreaded phone call suddenly awakes you during the night and you hear that grim voice on the other end share unexpected heartbreak. Or when you learn that your job is being outsourced, your bank account is dry, or the doctor has rendered a bad diagnosis.

No matter the source of the deluge, God has a purpose in the storm. It's our job to discern His purpose for us whether for our correction, spiritual growth, encouragement for ourselves or others. The only way we will discover His purpose is through His Word and seeking Him in prayer.

HEY LOOK, I'M WALKING ON THE WATER WITH JESUS

In Matthew 14:22-33 (Amplified Bible), we read the account of Jesus walking on the water during a terrible storm:

"Then He directed the disciples to get into the boat and go before Him to the other side, while He sent away the crowds. And after He had dismissed the multitudes, He went up into the hills by Himself to pray. When it was evening, He was still there alone.

But the boat was by this time out on the sea, many furlongs [a furlong is one-eighth of a mile] distant from the land, beaten and tossed by the waves, for the wind was against them. And in the fourth watch [between 3:00--6:00 a.m.] of the night, Jesus came to them, walking on the sea. And when the disciples saw Him walking on the sea, they were terrified and said, 'It is a ghost!' And they screamed out with fright. But instantly He spoke to them, saying, 'Take courage! I AM! Stop being afraid!'

And Peter answered Him, 'Lord, if it is You, command me to come to You on the water.' He said, 'Come!' So Peter got out of the boat and walked on the water, and he came toward Jesus. But when he perceived and felt the strong wind, he was frightened, and as he began to sink, he cried out, 'Lord, save me [from death]!'

Instantly Jesus reached out His hand and caught and held him, saying to him, 'O you of little faith, why did you doubt?' And when they got into the boat, the wind ceased. And those in the boat knelt and worshiped Him, saying, 'Truly You are the Son of God!'"

The disciples had just partaken in the miraculous feeding of the five thousand prior to Jesus sending them ahead by boat to the other side. Jesus telling them even though it was late, He would send away the multitude and also go alone on the mountain to pray.

Isn't it incredible that even to Jesus, the need to spend time alone with the Father was His main concern, although He probably was tired from an eventful afternoon of ministry and the crowd of people? He did not let the course of the day hinder Him from His relationship with God. He made the time. Unlike us when we are spent.

Then picture being in the boat with the disciples and listening to the "big fish-tale" they were rehashing with one another during their journey. They had just witnessed the Bread of Life feeding the immense crowd with just five loaves and two fish until all had eaten and were satisfied. Even taking up twelve baskets full of leftovers. *Amazing*!

But, when the disciples were mid-way in their travel, a horrific storm arose on the water; causing them to be tossed to and fro by the high waves from the pressing winds. Imagine trying to maneuver the boat against the turbulent sea as the waters over-lapped the sides of their vessel. *Can you say major anxiety and "sea sickness?"*

And although Jesus was not with them on the boat, He was well-aware of their plight in the over-whelming storm.

Did He intentionally send them ahead without Him to teach them another valuable lesson about the victory in the storm?

Visualize their surprise as they looked out on the unbearable waves and caught a glimpse of "some-one" walking on the tumultuous waters toward their periled vessel. But, instead of recognizing the Hope of all hopes, they became very frightened as they focused on their circumstance, thinking He was a ghost.

Foolish, fearful disciples. I can almost hear Jesus chuckle under His breath as He announced, *"Be of good cheer! It is I; do not be afraid."*

And I can almost feel His deep disappointment.

And once again, Peter jumps to the chance to prove "who" he was in Christ, crying out, *"Lord, if it is You, command me to come to You on the water."*

I wonder what his first initial thought really was when Jesus said, *"Come on".*

Isn't it ironic that Jesus had given Simon Peter the name *"Cephas,"* Aramaic for the Greek word *"Petros"* which means *"loose rock or stone?"* Without fail, Peter had been the most impulsive of the chosen twelve—at times, a "rock star" waiting to be discovered. His chief weakness—like us many times, His pride; however, God still used this flawed, ordinary fisherman for His extraordinary purpose many times. Peter became a "fisher of men."

Despite his imperfections, somehow Peter managed to throw his legs over the side of the tossed-about craft, climb out of the boat, and began walking on the water toward Jesus while the others watched, perhaps skeptically. Incredible!

"Hey look at me guys. I'm walking on the water with Jesus!"

However, like we all so often do, for an instant, Peter took his eyes off the Lord and put his focus back on the circumstance of the raging storm. Realizing that the wind was boisterous, once again, he became afraid – and he began to sink in the dark, churning waters of the squall, screaming out, *"Lord, save me!"*

As I contemplate this story, I wonder how come the other disciples didn't get out of the boat and also walk to Jesus on the water.

Could it be they were using human logic and felt safer staying within the security of the boat, even though it was being tossed about? Afraid to step out of their "comfort zone" into the unknown waters towards the Savior—trying to handle the outcome themselves.

Perhaps they were so consumed by their anxious conversations or the clamor of the storm that they could not hear Jesus bidding *them* to come.

Maybe others did not want to get their sandals wet. Possibly others couldn't swim.

Excuses when the Master bids us all *"Come."*

I try to envision the next part of this story in my own life—when immediately, Jesus stretched out his strong hands and caught Peter, and said to him, *"O you of little faith, why did you doubt?"*

It is not by coincident that after both had safely climbed into the boat, the storm stopped. *Powerful!*

Verse 33 goes on to say, *"Then those who were in the boat came and worshipped Him, saying, 'Truly You are the Son of God.'"*

Dynamic visual faith lesson. As we sail our own turbulent seas ("*C's*") of complacency, corruption, convenience, covetousness, complaining, etc., unable to recognize the Savior walking toward us in the storm.

How many gatherings, miracles, and lessons by the Master's hand would it take for them to fully understand? Most importantly, what will it take for us to get it?

While at a ladies conference at *Simpsonwood* in Norcross, Georgia, I was taken aback by the immense, wooden carving on the entryway of the conference center. It is a life-sized, raised, carved replica of Jesus with His hands actually reaching out to wearied travelers coming to renew their strength in Him at this beautiful retreat location.

Each time I entered the massive doors for meals or just to ponder His Word from a rocking chair on the back porch area before each session, I would first grasp hold of these outreached, wooden hands and close my eyes, trying to envision what it would be like if He truly were standing right there with His arms outstretched reaching out to mine.

Just to grab hold of the Savior's strong hand. I can only imagine. *And I can't wait!*

REFLECTIONS

I am thankful that God has a plan for us and many times He uses adversity and trials to slow us down and remind us that He has already won the battle. He has paid the price for each of us, yet we go day to day defeated, hard pressed, with our heads held down. It is no wonder that we cannot reach others with His hope because we act like we are carrying the weight of the world on our shoulders. We are so busy running our own race that we do not stop along the way to run with someone else. How can we share the fragrance of Christ with others when we are so saturated with the world's perfume?

When Mandi and Matt were small, I loved to hear them sing the chorus to "Victory in Jesus." Instead of singing, "He *plunged* me to victory beneath the cleansing flood," they proudly belted-out, "He *punched* me to victory."

During my recovery, I thought of how the enemy tries to rob us of God's victory and hope, and tarnish our testimony to others.

"Casting all your anxiety upon Him, because He careth for you. Be sober, be watchful: your adversary the devil, as a roaring lion, walketh about, seeking whom he may devour" (1 Peter 5:7-8, KJV).

I prayed I would not be a hindrance to anyone I came in contact with, even during this set-back I had experienced. I was aware others watched how I responded to this adversity. My reaction to the storm could either pull them to JESUS and His Hope or cause them to push further away!

How many times do we need to be punched to victory? Are we a testimony of defeat or triumph to those whose paths we cross? Can we proclaim Christ's victory boldly like the Apostle Paul, even when we're imprisoned with the shackles of our trials and illnesses? Are we faithful like Job, although he had lost everything, including his health and was ridiculed by his closest friends and wife, refused to curse God?

"But thanks be to God, which giveth us the victory through our Lord Jesus Christ" (1 Corinthians 15:57, KJV).

"I have trusted in Your faithful love; my heart will rejoice in Your deliverance" (Psalm 13:5, KJV).

GOD, OUR PROVIDER

Through my family, I am reminded daily of God's provision for us. As the parents of four children, we provided without question their shelter, food, clothing, entertainment, etc. They were born into our family! They have our name! They share our blood types! We know their voices, their likes, and even their dislikes. From the crib through college, we have been their providers.

Each of our children is unique, with varying gifts that complete our family. Our hearts truly praise God as we watch them grow and develop into the people He would have them to be. We've spent countless hours humbled on our knees in prayer for them and with them.

However, there have been those times when we have let them struggle—sometimes a little, sometimes a lot—to help them grow. There have also been occasions when we have had to discipline them to get them back on track. Through even the hard times, however, our love for them has never changed. It is unconditional!

When they have victories, we celebrate with them. When they are hurt and feel broken, we cry with them. We are still always available, although our role is somewhat different now that they are older and on their own.

"We have no greater joy than to know that each of them walks in God's truth!" (3 John 4, KJV).

"For this child I prayed: and the Lord hath given me my petition which I asked of Him. Therefore also I have lent him to the Lord; as long as he liveth he shall be lent to the Lord…" (1 Samuel 1:27–28, KJV).

When we accept Jesus as our Savior, we become God's children. We have His name! We are covered by His blood! Bought with a price! He wants to be our provision. He knows our likes and dislikes. He carries us through our struggles, and even during times of correction, He is there. He wants to celebrate our victories and comfort us when we hurt. He is always available to us. We are His! His love for us will never change. It is unconditional.

I can only imagine how it must grieve Him when we allow busy-ness to interfere with our fellowship with Him. When we choose the pleasures of the world over His Word and will for our lives. When we are too tired to pray and talk with Him…that is, until we need something and selfishly expect Him to answer quickly with the answer we anticipate.

Picture Larry and I not hearing from Mandi, Matt, John, or T.J. for months or even years until they are in need or crisis. Our hearts would be broken! This is what we do to our precious Father over and over again.

I recall an instance several years ago when I had prepared an extra special, full course meal on a Friday evening eagerly awaiting the arrival of one of our sons who was coming home from college for the weekend. I had made sure all his favorites were included in the menu. Hours passed and he had not come, so with a bruised spirit, I put all the goodies in the fridge. When my son finally arrived, he explained that he had stopped at a fast-food restaurant with friends instead, forgetting the feast that waited at home.

Isn't this just like us? God has prepared a feast for our lives, and we get sidetracked and settle for the fast food of the world. How it must break His heart as He waits for us to come to His table and we choose not to and make other plans. Why do we grab hold of the world's portion when God's provision is so much more appealing?

> "Surely He hath borne our griefs, and carried our sorrows…He was wounded for our transgressions, He was bruised for our iniquities: the chastisement of

our peace was upon Him; and with His stripes we are healed. All we like sheep have gone astray; we have turned every one to his own way; and the Lord hath laid on him the iniquity of us all" (Isaiah 53:4–6, KJV).

THE WAYWARD

He was known as the wayward son. The prodigal. Selfish and uncontrolled. I can hear the neighbors say what a disappointment he was to his father. "Have you heard about the problem son? Probably won't amount to much. Had the gall to expect his dad to give him his inheritance early, left home, and wasted everything by reckless living. Ended up in a pig pen."

I picture his father faithfully standing at the edge of his property, peering down the long, dirt road. Stretching his neck, intently looking, aching for the day his son would return home. Unable to concentrate on anything else except his missing child. Pondering where he had been. Was he safe? Would he ever come back? Watching. Waiting. Wondering. Probably worrying. And definitely praying.

Positioned at the border of his land like he had been time and time again, hoping this would be the day his son would return home, and finally catching a glimpse of someone familiar, head hung low, slowly coming up the long road. His heart smiled. It was his son.

It didn't matter where he had been or what he had done. It wasn't important what the neighbors had said about him. The prodigal had swallowed his pride, recognized his sin, and longed to be forgiven by his father. Expecting there might be a confrontation, the son rehearsed what he could say when he saw his dad, never imagining he would ever forgive him.

"Father, I have sinned against heaven, and against thee, and am no more worthy to be called thy son: make me as one of thy hired servants" (Luke 15:18–19, KJV).

Nevertheless, to his father all that counted was the sight of his son coming toward him. Not able to wait any longer, he ran to meet his lost son. Embraced him. Loved him. Forgave him. More than the son could ever have hoped for. What a celebration!

"But when he was yet a great way off, his father saw him, and had compassion, and ran, and fell on his neck, and kissed him...For this my son was dead, and is alive again; he was lost, and is found. And they began to be merry" (Luke 15:20, 24, KJV).

We have all been prodigals. Making demands on our heavenly Father to give us what we think we deserve. We've squandered our gifts, wasted our time, ran away from Him, and embraced the world. Even though He knows and sees all we have done, He still loves us, although our rebellion breaks His heart.

Faithfully, He stands with His arms outstretched toward us. Watching and waiting for us to come back home. Moreover, He forgives when we finally realize how our separation has hurt Him. Undeservingly, He runs to embrace us! More than we could ever have hoped for.

WE CANNOT BECOME HIS MESSENGER UNTIL WE GO THROUGH THE MESS

Okay, so you may be ready to give up. You're tired of the muddle. Like me, finding His purpose in the mess is of utmost importance. *Remember:*

- We don't have a testimony until we experience the test. There is someone God wants you to touch through your struggle. Praise Him for this opportunity!

- We need to stop trying to eat all of life's pie at one sitting and chew through it one slice at a time…savor each bite!

- We must never let failure and disappointments set our course of life. Try to find something positive in each struggle. Victory is just around the corner. The worst storms make the best rainbows!

- Never allow discouragement to overtake your faith in Him. Remember, He sees the whole picture! His strength is perfect when we are our weakest.

- Do not allow those who have no faith to influence the outcome. Surround yourself with positive prayer warriors and take a vacation from negative friends. Find something to laugh about together.

- Do not give place to pettiness and hold on to token possessions above serving Him. Even our most cherished possessions are temporary and eventually will need to be repaired or replaced. Relationship is everlasting.
- Faith knows the nature of the battle. Recall previous victories when you get down.
- Pray without ceasing! Meditate on His Word. Be still and listen to Him.
- *Physically,* get off the couch and exercise at least thirty minutes a day. Take a walk! Eat healthier. Eat less trans and saturated fats. Know your cholesterol levels and blood pressure. Have a yearly check-up and lab work.

DO YOU KNOW HIM?

As a young man, Mylon R. Lefevre, a Southern gospel singer who has appeared with the Gaithers, wrote one of the most pertinent songs about our need for Jesus as our Savior, "Without Him":[8]

Without Him I could do nothing,
Without Him I'd surely fail;
Without Him I would be drifting,
Like a ship without a sail
Jesus, O Jesus, Do you know
Him today?
Do not turn Him away!
O Jesus, O Jesus, Without Him
How lost I would be
Without Him, I would be dying,
Without Him I'd be enslaved;
Without Him life would be hopeless—
But with Jesus, Thank God I'm saved.
Jesus, O Jesus, Do you know
Him today?
Do not turn Him away!

O Jesus, O Jesus, Without Him
How lost I would be

In May 1982, as an active member at Fellowship Baptist Church, in the small gulf-side town of Carrabelle, Florida, I accepted Jesus Christ as my Lord and Savior. The irony of my salvation experience is that I was the church secretary, taught Vacation Bible School, helped Larry teach the youth in Sunday school, and each Sunday stood in front of the whole church congregation, presenting a well-orchestrated children's sermon before our pastor came with his message. It seemed I was in church each time the toilet flushed or the door opened.

My best friends were dynamic Christians, so I knew all the correct Christian jargon and could rattle off inspirational prayers and Bible verses easily. I made sure I was part of each women's Bible study group. No one suspected that I did not have a real relationship with Christ, that is, until a visiting pastor came to preach revival.

I am not sure how he recognized I was a fake, but almost immediately upon our first encounter, he challenged my salvation. I was taken aback that he did not believe I knew Christ as my Savior, and dragging Mandi and Matt out the door, we abruptly left the church for the day. I informed Larry when he got home that I would not be going back to church until the revival was over. Who did this minister think he was?

As we all do when we think we are wronged, I called two of my closest friends. The first, my pastor's wife, said I must have misunderstood. After all, this man did not know me and all the good things I did in the church. At the end of our conversation, she confirmed what a great a person I thought I was.

However, when I called my other friend, she surprised me when she said I would not be having such a struggle if I were not under conviction. I slammed the phone down! Who did she think she was? Miss Holier-Than-Thou.

I was expecting our third child and decided to use my tiredness as an excuse to skip revival services. In spite of this, Larry had other plans and told me that we would be going to church as a family. No excuses.

In my mind I thought, *You can make me go, but you can't make me listen.* Thus, like one of my children might do, I doodled on a scrap of paper throughout the message. Even with my stubbornness, God had other plans, too!

I am not sure what the moment was for me, but I knew in my heart that Jesus was not my Savior. I had been relying on my church membership, works, good deeds, and the affirmation of how great I was in place of what Jesus had done for me. I positively, without a doubt, knew at that moment if I had died before that day, I would have spent eternity in hell separated from my Father.

As the visiting minister was ending his sermon, he paused. Without delay, I stood up and immediately proceeded down the aisle towards him. "You were right!" I exclaimed as I journeyed to the altar. Almost audibly, I heard a surprised sigh from the congregation. No one could believe that such a nice person had been lost!

I wanted to be baptized immediately, this time for real. I was seven months pregnant and rather large. As my minister and a deacon lowered me under the water, he stated with a chuckle he had never baptized two for the price of one.

I finally had the true assurance of salvation through Jesus Christ I had been working so hard to find. With a smile in my heart, I could feel God say, "This is my beloved daughter, in whom I am well pleased."

While at cardiac rehab walking on the treadmill, I had an epiphany concerning salvation. No matter what speed I set my pace on the treadmill, whether fast or slow, once I step back onto the floor, I end up at the exact same place I started my workout. I have not gone anywhere even though I have been walking for twenty-five minutes and sometimes break a sweat. It is useless for me to hope the treadmill will get me to my desired destination. It can't.

Salvation is not based on our feelings, emotions, works, or goodness, but only on what Christ did for us. He paid the penalty for our sinful nature. It cost Him His life! His shed blood! It doesn't matter that we come from a strong Christian family, are members of a church, or have been baptized. It doesn't help that we tithe, go on visitation, or give to the poor. There is not one good thing we can do to earn our salvation. If our salvation experience is based on anything other than Christ, we are lost.

When I needed to have the blockages in my heart repaired, I sought a heart specialist to do the surgery. I did not ask my dentist or family physician for their assistance. Since heart surgery was not their specialty, they could not help me. I wanted someone who knew everything necessary to fix my heart. A heart authority.

In order to repair our broken, sinful hearts, we cannot go to anyone else but Jesus, the Heart Authority. There is no other person or thing that can save us, no matter how good the remedy sounds or makes us feel.

"I am the Way, the Truth, and the Life: no man cometh unto the Father; but by Me" (John 14:6, KJV).

I have been burdened thinking how many good people—like I was—may sit in the church pew Sunday after Sunday, year after year, and do not know Jesus as their Savior, and play the game. They do the works. Smile the smile. However, they're still lost.

I sadly imagine those that believe they are beyond His help. Toting too much baggage to be forgiven of their sins. Thinking it is too late. Ashamed to come before Him for salvation. Worried they are not worthy. Not knowing that He died for them just the way they are, baggage and all. Could you be one of them?

- *Stop comparing yourself to others. Compared to our Holy Father, we are all guilty.*

"For all have sinned and come short of the glory of God" (Romans 3:23, KJV).

"There is none righteous, no, not one" (Romans 3:10, KJV).

- *It doesn't matter how nice we are…we cannot save ourselves by being good or doing good works—eternal life is a free gift through Jesus Christ.*

"For by grace are you saved, through faith; and that not of yourselves: it is a gift of God: Not of works, lest any man should boast" (Ephesians 2:8–9, KJV).

"For the wages of sin is death, but the gift of God is eternal life through Jesus Christ our Lord" (Romans 6:23, KJV).

- *You need the heart knowledge and not just head knowledge. Believing facts about God will not save us—we must place our faith in Him.*

"You believe that there is one God: You do well: the devils also believe, and tremble" (James 2:19, KJV).

- *Admit it! We must confess Jesus as Lord and repent of our sins.*

"That if thou shalt confess with thy mouth the Lord Jesus, and shalt believe in thine heart that God hath raised Him from the dead, thou shalt be saved. For with the heart man believeth unto righteousness; and with the mouth confession is made unto salvation" (Romans 10:9–10, KJV).

"Repent ye therefore, and be converted, that your sins may be blotted out" (Acts 3:19, KJV).

"I, even I, am He that blotteth out thy transgressions for mine own sake, and will not remember thy sins" (Isaiah 43:25, KJV).

REJOICE

"For God so loved the world that He gave His only begotten Son, that whosoever believeth in Him should not perish, but have everlasting life" (John 3:16, KJV).

I know. It's hard to believe, but you are the "whosoever" He died for. If there had been no one else but you on the earth, He would have still gone to the cross for you. He loves you. He waits for you. So what are you waiting for?

"Behold, now is the day of salvation" (2 Corinthians 6:2, KJV).

Pray this simple prayer today to receive your gift of salvation:

Lord Jesus,
I know you are the Son of God and died to forgive me of my sins. I am a sinner and have ignored Your purpose for me. I know I cannot save myself. You are my only hope. Please forgive me from my sins. I turn

away from them and I receive you as my Lord and Savior. Thank you for paying the price by dying on the cross and saving me. Amen

I HAVE CALLED YOU BY NAME

We've allowed ourselves to be consumed by the world's status quo and forget that we are precious in His sight. Instead we place our focus on obtaining things that are temporary and give us immediate gratification. Think about it. We are owned by what we possess.

Ironically, when the novelty of the purchase subsides, we are still left empty apart from Him. Fancy houses eventually need repair, cleaning, and painting. Once the new car smell is gone, it's just a car and no longer brings us the satisfaction it did when it was new. So why do we store up for ourselves "treasures on earth, where moth and rust destroy, and where thieves break in and steal" (Matthew 6:19, KJV)?

We are His children. He calls us by name. "Talk to me, _____," He pleads. Yet, we go on this day-to-day journey by ourselves, struggling to bear the load.

> "Fear not: for I have redeemed thee. I have called thee by thy name; thou art mine. When thou passest through the

waters, I will be with thee: and through the rivers, they shall not overflow thee: when thou walkest through the fire, thou shalt not be burned; neither shall the flame kindle upon thee. For I am the Lord thy God, the Holy One of Israel, thy Savior. Since thou was precious in my sight...Fear not: for I am with thee" (Isaiah 43:1–5, KJV).

Through my recent heart encounter, I have realized we must cherish each day and the people God places before us. Life can change with each heartbeat. This moment we hold is a precious possession. Every person in our path is a blessing that we may not have a chance to experience again.

Time is a gift and we live with many regrets because we will not slow down and cherish what we are given. We've taken for granted the blessings of life and each other, and do not savor precious moments.

We have it all, yet possess nothing when we allow ourselves to be robbed of the fragrance of relationship with Him and others because we have become so busy trying to survive the rat race.

God has written all chapters in the story of our life. He has woven each unique detail about who we are and His purpose for us. We may not be sure what tomorrow is going to bring, but He holds all our tomorrows.

In Matthew 10:30 (KJV), He tells us, "the very hairs of our head are all numbered." If He cares about even the smallest areas of our lives, why do we worry about the future?

He understands all our needs, even before we do. No matter where we go, He is there. We cannot escape His love for us. He is able to do "exceeding abundantly above all that we ask or think, according to the power that works in us" (Ephesians 3:20, KJV), so why do we get so anxious?

Again I am reminded the Father wants to go on this heart journey with me. He wants to clear the broken pieces from my path. He wants to take care of the hidden obstacles that pop up in my life. He wants to hold the flashlight in the darkness. He wants me to climb on His lap during the storm.

Most importantly, He wants to do the same for you. Once more, what are you waiting for? What will it take?

ME AND MY EPIPHANY MOMENTS

One Sunday morning, I was asked by our interim pastor to share some updated information about our church's volunteer cancer ministry called "*hope*" with my church family.

I was one of the volunteers of this vital outreach and I was probably one of the most vocal about the importance of this ministry and those affected by cancer, including family members and friends, whose lives our church had touched.

I no longer have the much-needed stamina to perform the necessary physical tasks to meet care receiver requests, such as: cleaning houses, yard work, meals, etc., but I have been endowed in the "gift of gab" area, and I love to encourage. So when asked to say something to the church about the progress of the program, I jumped (*okay leaped carefully*), at a chance to share something near and dear to my heart... reaching out to others with His Hope in times of their despair.

By the way, speaking of hearts—on the outside, although I move slower and tire easily, I look fine, but that particular morning, on the inside I was experiencing an "on again and off again" bout of angina pain. Still smiling and acting normal (*okay, normal for me*), no one including Larry, knew the discomfort that was occurring in my chest.

Just me — and a war of denial kept playing over and over in my head as I attempted to ignore my symptoms as I spoke, even though I knew better.

At the end of the service, several people came up to me and remarked how wonderful it was to see me looking so healthy since my earlier journey with heart surgery and its complications. And I continued to smile and deny (*I have developed this skill rather well*).

However, others could not see the two, new heart blockages also unknown to me, that could develop into possible hindrances to my life ... But, God was aware.

And early the next morning, after Larry had left for his office, and following unsuccessful attempts to rid my chest pain with three more nitroglycerin tablets, I contacted my cardiologist's office, again, making excuses even to her of the possible causes of the pain. *"Pulled chest muscle? Gas? Something I ate?"*

"Put your shoes on—get in the car, and come to the Heart Center," she responded, "just as a precaution to make sure nothing major is going on, I want to do a catheterization this morning."

As she requested without thinking, I put on my tennis shoes and drove myself the twenty-five miles down I-75 to the hospital. *Yep, alone!*

Pulling into the parking deck, I became a little uneasy about not letting Larry know what was going on, and thought it probably would be a smart idea to call him at work and subtly let him know what had transpired. I was going to have catheterization and he probably needed to be aware.

"Hey, Dr. Jones is going to do cath on me as a precaution for some angina pain I've been having."

"What day are you having it?" he questioned.

Trying to act unconcerned I answered, "I am in the parking deck of the Medical Center right now. She wants to do the procedure this morning after I am prepped."

"Who drove you to the hospital?"

"Well…"

Our silence echoed loudly in my ear.

"I'll be right there." Click.

Praying he wasn't aggravated, alone I walked myself into the large registration lobby—where they were expecting me. Because I have been there so often, checking into the heart center was a fast procedure, and I entered the elevator to the cath floor quicker than I had anticipated.

After being prepped, Larry and our oldest son, Matt arrived. Shortly, I was wheeled into the cath lab.

The security of its familiarity, including the lab techs, anesthesiologists, plus my cardiologist were a comfort. Casual conversation began, until my doctor questioned me about how I arrived at the hospital since she had *recently* passed Larry rushing down the hall toward my room.

Can you say a mini-lecture by her ensued for my foolish travel alone up the interstate while I was experiencing undiagnosed angina pain? I had not even considered I could have been having a heart attack, putting myself or other drivers in possible peril.

During the course of our discussion, I underwent two angioplasty procedures and two failed stent attempts for the new clogs. It wasn't a big area like the four obstructions before, but had the potential of causing further damage if left untreated and allowed to worsen.

Amazingly, sometimes it is the smallest things that get us into trouble if left untreated, both physically and spiritually.

Following the procedure, our interim minister came by the hospital.

"It is incredible that we could not tell there was anything wrong with your heart while you spoke to the congregation yesterday," he inserted.

Simultaneously, in my hospital room, we both received an epiphany moment of what I needed to do the following Sunday; and six-days later, I walked to the front of the congregation, and began to share what had gone on with my heart without their awareness.

As I gazed out toward my church family, with care, I began to speak:

"There is urgency in my heart for my church family today. Looking out in the congregation, most of you are smiling; some of you are deacons, directors, teachers, Sunday school and choir members. Most of you even carry your Bibles. Some of you never miss a worship or prayer service.

In my mind I think what a wonderful group of dynamic Christians you all appear to be. Foolishly, I presume that because you look so good on the outside and do the right 'churchy' things, inside, you must have a genuine relationship with Jesus. Sadly, I can't see what is actually going on in your hearts—BUT GOD CAN.

1 Samuel 16:7(NKJV) says, 'For the Lord does not see as man sees; for man looks at the outward appearance, but the Lord looks at the heart.'

Last Sunday I stood before you sharing about our "hope" volunteer cancer ministry. Several of you remarked how well I looked, but you couldn't see the conflict that was going on inside my heart, and the next morning, I was at the Medical Center undergoing a cath and angio procedure.

Just as only my heart specialist could take care of the blockages and physical damage to my heart this week and in the past, Jesus, our Heart Authority is the only One who can eternally repair our broken and sinful hearts.

Isn't it sad how the smallest ills of life have the greatest potential to cause us the most harm? When we allow our hearts to become clogged with sin, worry, unforgiveness, pride, bitterness, jealousy, hatred, and anger?

I ponder, if there are any of you, my precious church family, who sit in the pew Sunday after Sunday, who do not really know Jesus as your personal Savior. You play the game, but you do not have the assurance of what Christ alone did for you at Calvary, by paying the penalty for your sins. It cost Him His life! If your salvation is based on anything other than Jesus, sadly you are lost.

In John 14:6 (NKJV), Jesus said, 'I am the Way, the Truth, and the Life. No one comes to the Father except through Me.'

So, what is your 'hope' built on? Your position, church membership, how good you are, how much you tithe? Or is it built on nothing less than Jesus and His righteousness? It is only by His grace through faith that you are saved.

You know, I could have ignored the heart symptoms I was experiencing and suffered the consequences that could have resulted in my physical death. I wonder if any of you are ignoring the Holy Spirit's call to the true salvation found only in Jesus Christ and risking the consequence of eternal death.

2 Corinthians 6:2(NKJV) says, 'Behold, now is the day of salvation.'

I don't know about my tomorrows—but I know the ONE who holds them. How about you? Just as my heart condition was sudden and unexpected, you may face eternity unexpectedly. What will be the condition of your heart"?

When I was finished sharing, I went back to my seat weeping and broken, praying that they got it.

Do you?

A FRAGRANT AFTERTHOUGHT

Family members enthusiastically cram the confines of a labor room, all in eager anticipation of the arrival of a new life, Matt and Candice's second child. When it appears that both mother and baby might be experiencing a little distress, we do not hesitate to surround Candice's bed, joining hearts in bonded prayer believing God already has His hand on this precious life.

At last, Luke makes his welcomed appearance amid our *oo's* and *ah's*. Celebration and thanksgiving resound throughout the hospital floor flavored with hugs and tears. Elatedly, we quickly dial our cell phones, sharing each intricate detail about Luke's new life with those absent from the blessed event. We cannot contain the joy of his birth!

As I peer into the eyes of my oldest son, now the father of two, I marvel at his pride and excitement as he closely examines each tiny finger and toe. Once again, the hand of the Master touches my heart as He reminds me, although hard to comprehend, how much *more joy and celebration there is in Heaven* when a life is born into the family of God...changed by what Jesus did at Calvary. The moment we are no longer outsiders bound by sin, but become children of the King of kings!

Already knowing each finger and toe, God looks upon the repented heart. Elatedly, sharing each intricate detail with the heavenly hosts. He cannot contain the joy of this new birth. Moreover, the joy of heaven resounds with Him!

"I say unto you, that likewise joy shall be in heaven over one sinner that repenteth, more than over ninety and nine just persons, which need no repentance...Likewise, I say unto you, there is joy in the presence of the angels of God over one sinner that repenteth" (Luke 15:7–8, KJV).

"But as many as received him, to them gave he power to become the sons of God even to them that believe on his name" (John 1:12, KJV).

"That being justified by his grace, we should be made heirs according to the hope of eternal life" (Titus 3:7, KJV).

When was the last time we were stirred by another's birth in Christ? Has our joy become so contained, soured by our complacency and indifference as we concentrate more on the world's tasks that lay ahead of us instead of the excitement of new birth in Him? Sorrowfully, I contemplate those occasions when I was more concerned with my own agenda than the eternity of another's.

Preceding Luke's birth, Candice meticulously readied even the smallest area of his new home with precision as she anxiously counted down the days before his arrival. No corner was left untouched by her hand.

God reminded me how He is also preparing a place for us. Our eternal home! Readying even the smallest detail with precision. Anxiously counting down the days before our arrival in Glory! No area left untouched by the Master's hand. What a day that will be!

> "Let not your heart be troubled: ye believe in God, believe also in me. In my Father's house are many mansions: if it were not so, I would have told you. I go to prepare a place for you. And if I go and prepare a place for you, I will come again, and receive you unto myself; that where I am, there ye may be also" (John 14:1–3, KJV).

I cannot envision what it will be like to humbly stand before my Heavenly Father. To see the face of the One who paid the price for me. To finally end earth's journey of the heart as I join those who have gone home before me. The moment I catch sight of loved ones that I have missed so badly. A celebration beyond my comprehension.

"And God shall wipe away all tears from their eyes; and there shall be no more death, neither sorrow, nor crying, neither shall there be any more pain: for the former things are passed away" (Revelation 21:4, KJV).

God will not be impressed with how many reports I finished at work, how much money I had in the bank, or how big my house was. What will matter most to Him is what I did with Jesus during my journey. Did I take the time to share His hope with those who felt hopeless? Or place as much significance on a lost soul as I did on a lost set of keys?

I will also give an account of what I did with unforeseen detours that popped up before me. Did I tightly grasp my Savior's hand and allow Him to direct my path? Or stomp away like an angry child when facing uncertain delays and pitfalls, ignoring His direction for my life?

I have learned not to be afraid of an unexpected bypass in the road. Until I surrendered to my uncertain path, I did not discover how God was paving the way using this adversity to open the door to fulfill a forgotten dream in my life. The desire to write.

Long before you opened this book, I prayed for you. I prayed you would not grow weary on your journey and would realize His hope even though your situation might seem hopeless. That you would allow Him to fill the emptiness or fear you might be experiencing. Remember, YOU are not alone. He wants to wipe away the tears from your eyes.

This is not just my story, but also His story. The victory that can only be found through Jesus Christ. My sincere wish is that His hand will touch your life as never before, even in the impossible. Again, don't give up! Traveling off the beaten path yields the most beautiful scenery if we allow God to lead our journey of the heart!

"That the name of our Lord Jesus Christ may be glorified in you" (2 Thessalonians 1:12, KJV).

ENDNOTES:
ON-LINE REFERENCES

1   Merriam-Webster Online Dictionary. "Journey." January 15, 2007. http://www.m-w.com/

2   American Heart Association Homepage. "Learn and Live" February 8, 2007. http://www.american-heart.org

3   WebMD Website. "Your Blood Pressure Goal." February 8, 2007. http://www.webmd.com/

4   American Heart Association Website. "Cholesterol Levels." AHA Recommendation. February 8, 2007. http://www.americanheart.org/cholesterol

5   American Heart Association Website. "Physical Activity." Search/AHA Scientific Position. February 8, 2007. http://www.americanheart.org

6   American Heart Association Website. "Heart Attack Warning Signs." January 15, 2007. http://www.americanheart.org

7   CBN Partner Elaine. "Re: Prayer Request–Healing." March 2, 2007. CBNPartnerRepElaine@cbn.org

8   WITHOUT HIM/ Mylon Lefevre/ Angel Band Music/ BMI/ Administered by Gaither Copyright Management/ Used by Permission.